JOSSEY-BASS GUIDES
TO ONLINE TEACHING AND LEARNING

Engaging the Online Learner

Updated

Activities and Resources for Creative Instruction

Rita-Marie Conrad

J. Ana Donaldson

JOSSEY-BASS
A Wiley Imprint
www.josseybass.com

Published by Jossey-Bass
A Wiley Imprint
989 Market Street, San Francisco, CA 94103-1741—www.josseybass.com

Jossey-Bass books and products are available through most bookstores. To contact Jossey-Bass directly call our Customer Care Department within the U.S. at 800-956-7739, outside the U.S. at 317-572-3986, or fax 317-572-4002.

Jossey-Bass also publishes its books in a variety of electronic formats. Some content that appears in print may not be available in electronic books.

Library of Congress Cataloging-in-Publication Data

Conrad, Rita-Marie.
 Engaging the online learner : activities and resources for creative instruction / Rita-Marie Conrad, J. Ana Donaldson. – Updated ed.
  p. cm. – (Jossey-bass guides to online teaching and learning)
  Includes bibliographical references and index.
 ISBN 978-1-118-01819-4 (pbk.)
 ISBN 978-1-118-05934-0 (ebk.)
 ISBN 978-1-118-05936-4 (ebk.)
 ISBN 978-1-118-05982-1 (ebk.)
 1. Inclusive education. 2. Computer-assisted instruction. 3. Education–Effect of technological innovations on. 4. Digital electronics. I. Donaldson, J. Ana. II. Title.
 LB1028.5.C623 2011
 371.33'4–dc22

                                                                                    2011001415

Printed in the United States of America
FIRST EDITION
PB Printing 10 9 8 7 6 5 4 3 2

Contents

Preface

Experts in online learning have repeatedly written that both learners and instructors have new roles to fulfill in an online learning environment. A major challenge facing online educators is not only how to become better facilitators of knowledge acquisition but also how to help learners become more self-directed and collaborative with peers than they might have had to be in traditional, predominantly lecture-based courses. How can an instructor energize a learning environment and empower learners to adopt responsibility for their own learning? How can this be done without verbal or physical communication cues in an environment where it is easy to hide from the instructor and peers?

While educators and learners in classroom-based courses have already discovered the benefits of an engaged learning approach to education, the power of engagement in online courses is yet to be fully realized. We define engaged learning as a collaborative learning process in which the instructor and learner are partners in building the knowledge base. The use of online interactive tools such as asynchronous discussion boards and synchronous chats by educators initially began about twenty years ago. The publication of strategies and guidelines concerning how to use online communication tools to build learning communities began with Harasim, Hiltz, Teles, and Turoff's book *Learning Networks* (1996), which was followed a few years later by Palloff and Pratt's *Building Learning Communities in Cyberspace* (1999), Salmon's *e-tivities* (2002) and then our first edition of *Engaging the Online Learner* in 2004.

Why another book on the topic of online interaction and engagement? This book represents an alternative for online practitioners who are looking for new ideas to enhance their online instruction, providing another framework to consider when designing and implementing online interaction. The proposed framework helps instructors guide learners in the development of skills needed to engage with the content and with one another online without the instructor being the primary initiator of knowledge generation and interaction. We perceived a need for such a framework in our own work as online instructors and in various workshops we conducted with other online instructors. All of us seemed to be seeking methods to improve learner interaction online. Through our experiences it became clear that we could not assume that learners knew how to interact online and how to become more responsible for their online learning. We could not become "guides on the side" without learners becoming more involved as knowledge generators and cofacilitators of the course. The Phases of Engagement framework was developed to help resolve these issues.

While the framework will be of help in explaining how to ease learners into their new role, the strength of this book lies in the numerous examples of activities provided by experienced online instructors across the nation. These activities illustrate various ways in which engaged learning can be promoted in an online environment. While there are many elements that contribute to a successful online course, we have chosen to focus solely on activities because many courses are moving from an instructor-centered, lecture-based focus to a collaborative, learner-centered focus, and the architects of online courses need ideas on how to make this shift occur smoothly.

We do not intend to delve deeply into the theory of engaged learning. Rather, we seek to provide a means to apply that theory in the online environment through various types of activities as represented by the work of others who have successfully infused principles of engagement into their online courses.

The intended audience of the book is practitioners who are relatively new to the online learning environment or who are dealing with learners who are relatively new to online coursework. We also hope this book will be helpful to experienced online practitioners who are seeking inspiration for their established online activities.

OVERVIEW OF THE CONTENTS

The book consists of two parts. Part One provides a basic framework with which to organize activities so that engagement is introduced into the online environment and learned by community members in phases. Chapter One provides an overview of the components necessary for engaged learning as well as a framework for building the trust and interdependence needed for learners to interact and learn their new role in an engaged online environment. Chapter Two discusses how to convert your classroom activities to an online environment and how to choose an effective online communication tool. Chapter Three addresses how to assess the learning that occurs as a result of collaborative activities. Interactivity may be high in an online learning environment, but what was actually learned may not be immediately apparent. This chapter provides guidelines for developing assessments for the types of activities discussed in this book.

Part Two presents activities that can be used to promote engagement among online learners on a phase-by-phase basis. Use them as they are or adapt them to more closely fit your subject matter. Chapters Four through Ten describe specific types of activities keyed to each phase of engagement and provide several examples of each type. Each activity contains the title and the name of the instructor who tested the activity in an online environment and submitted it for inclusion in the book. Chapter Four focuses on how to help learners learn to use online tools. Chapter Five provides examples of online icebreakers. Chapter Six discusses building peer interaction through peer partnerships and team activities. In Chapter Seven, the use of reflective activities is the focus. Chapter Eight provides examples of authentic activities. Chapter Nine focuses on games and simulations. Chapter Ten discusses learner-led activities.

UPDATES

This revised edition includes updated references, additional notes on the use of the activities, and the implications of new technology tools. We believe the original activities are still relevant and therefore remain intact. These activities are also useful in a blended learning environment, which has become more prevalent since this book was first published. New activities will be presented in an upcoming book.

ACKNOWLEDGMENTS

This book presents not only our ideas but those of numerous faculty across the United States who have creatively and diligently worked to engage online learners. We salute the faculty members who volunteered their activities for use in this book. It has indeed been a community endeavor, and we are deeply indebted to each contributor.

A special thanks goes to Bill Draves and the LERN organization for helping us to reach faculty nationwide. We are particularly grateful to Rena Palloff and Keith Pratt, who inspired us and encouraged us. Without them, this book would not have come to fruition. Our gratitude also goes to Rhonda Robinson and Sharon Smaldino for their mentorship, to Belle Cowden for her contribution to the development of the phases of engagement and to the director and staff of the Annual Conference on Distance Teaching and Learning in Madison, Wisconsin, who provided the environment in which this book was conceived and nurtured. Our deep appreciation also goes to David Brightman, Cathy Mallon, and Erin Null, our editors at Jossey-Bass.

And to the most important people in our lives, our families, we express our deepest gratitude—to Larry and Alec Conrad for their understanding, patience and abiding belief, and to Al Donaldson for his encouragement, love, and shared laughter.

AN INVITATION

Please let us know how you use the activities in this book. Also, if you have an activity that you would like to share in future editions, please contact Rita at rconrad@nc.rr.com or Ana at ana.donaldson@cfu.net. We look forward to hearing from you.

Rita-Marie Conrad   J. Ana Donaldson
Chapel Hill, North Carolina   *Cedar Falls, Iowa*

The Authors

Rita-Marie Conrad has been teaching, designing and consulting about online courses for nearly two decades. She was the head of online instructional development and an online faculty member in the School of Information Studies at Florida State University. She also assisted in the development of two master's programs in Instructional Systems in the FSU College of Education and was an online faculty member for those programs as well. Conrad consults on the design, implementation, and evaluation of online courses, and provides training to community college and university faculty. She is a frequent presenter on the topic of online instruction at various national forums such as the Learning Resources Network (LERN) and the Annual Conference on Distance Teaching and Learning. Conrad has also taught online courses for Walden University, Fielding Graduate Institute, Capella University, and Nova Southeastern University. She is coauthor of the *Faculty Guide to Moving Teaching and Learning to the Web, The Online Teaching Survival Guide*, and *Assessing Learners Online.*

Conrad has a bachelor's degree in accounting from Illinois State University and a master's degree in educational media and computers from Arizona State University. She holds a Ph.D. in instructional systems from Florida State University.

J. Ana Donaldson retired as an associate professor of instructional technology from the University of Northern Iowa. She continues her love of teaching online by working part time as a contributing faculty member for Walden University. She also provides instructional design and program evaluation consulting. For many years, she has presented workshops on how to effectively use technology to apply the principles of engaged learning in the classroom and online.

Besides her years of classroom experience in creating Web-supported learning environments, Donaldson is a published author, keynote speaker, and international presenter. She has presented at conferences sponsored by the International Visual Literacy Association, the University of Wisconsin, the Association for Educational Communication and Technology, and the International Conference on Education Research on a variety of engaged learning topics.

Donaldson received a bachelor's degree in computer science and a master's degree in instructional technology from Northern Illinois University. She holds an Ed.D. in instructional technology from Northern Illinois University. She has been elected the 2011–2012 AECT (Association for Educational Communication and Technology) president.

Engaging the Online Learner

Updated

Learning in an Online Environment

*Learners in the twenty-first century have been Web consumers
for much of their lives, and are now demanding online
instruction that supports participation and interaction.
They want learning experiences that are social and that
will connect them with their peers.*

West & West, 2009, p. 2

Engaged learning is not a new instructional approach. It has been written about under various terms such as *active learning, social cognition, constructivism*, and *problem-based learning*, all of which emphasize student-focused learning within an instructor-facilitated environment.

A century ago, Dewey recognized the importance of active learning with the instructor in a supportive role as a facilitator. Dewey (1916/1997) emphasized the value of the individual experience in the learning process as well as collaboration with others in order to define the learning environment. Dewey's work was predominantly in the primary and secondary school environment but was extended to adult learners by Malcolm Knowles's concept of andragogy (1980), which considers the adult learner to be self-directed and desirous of an active learning environment in which his or her own experiences play a part.

Other learning theorists such as Bruner, Vygotsky, and Piaget all embraced the philosophy that humans do not learn in a vacuum but rather through interaction. Bruner in his work with Bornstein (1989) stated that "development is intrinsically bound up with interaction" (p. 13), which built on his earlier definition of reciprocity as the "deep human need to respond to others and to operate jointly with them toward an objective" (Bruner, 1966, p. 67).

Vygotsky (1981) believed that social interaction helped students learn from the viewpoints of others in order to build a more complex worldview. One of the cornerstones of Vygotsky's work is the "zone of proximal development," which is the difference between the problem-solving ability of an individual independently and the individual's potential ability when working with an adult or more advanced peer. Vygotsky saw instruction as effective only if it stimulated those abilities and helped the learner across the zone of proximal development.

Piaget's philosophy emphasized that learning must be connected to the learner in order to be meaningful (Piaget, 1969). He described engaged learning (constructivism was his term of choice) as how we come to know our world, with knowledge built on prior experiences and affected by new experiences. Unlike Vygotsky, Piaget proposed that development would be more likely to occur when two equal partners collaborated in finding a solution than when a more skilled partner dominated the task. Piaget believed effective discussions were only possible when there was symmetrical power between the discussants. Peer-to-peer discussion was more valuable than adult-to-child discussion because equals were more likely to resolve the contradictions between each other's views than were partners of unequal authority.

The emergence of problem-based learning (PBL) was an evolutionary step along the engaged learning continuum. In a PBL environment, a problem is posed to learners who work together in teams to define the nature of the problem and determine its resolution. Through this process, learners can "develop intellectual curiosity, confidence and engagement that will lead to lifelong learning" (Watson

& Groh, 2001, p. 21). As with the work that preceded it, PBL is based on interaction and meaningful learning.

Although interaction is a thread that runs through many learning theories, constructivism considers it central to learning and addresses epistemology within the context of the individual and within social constructs. According to Smith and Ragan, (1999, p. 15), the key assumptions of individual constructivism are the following:

- Knowledge is constructed from experience.
- Learning results from a personal interpretation of knowledge.
- Learning is an active process in which meaning is developed on the basis of experience.
- Learning is collaborative with meaning negotiated from multiple perspectives.

This collaborative acquisition of knowledge is one key to the success of creating an online learning environment. Activities that require student interaction and encourage a sharing of ideas promote a deeper level of thought.

In his summary of social constructivism, Weigel (2002) cautions that focusing on content acquisition defeats the overall purpose of education. "Content is the clay of knowledge construction; learning takes place when it is fashioned into something meaningful. Creativity, critical analysis, and skillful performance are inextricably linked to the process of creating more viable and coherent knowledge structures" (p. 5). In the online environment, collaborative activities are what allow the clay to take form and have meaning for the learner.

As illustrated in Figure 1.1, the combination of constructivist and problem-based learning philosophies within a collaborative context result in an engaged learning environment. Engaged learning is focused on the learner, whose role is integral to the generation of new knowledge. In an engaged learning environment, each learner's actions contribute not only to individual knowledge but to overall community knowledge development as well.

Must you be an adamant constructivist to believe in learner engagement? No. As Collison, Elbaum, Haavind, and Tinker (2000) point out, "There is strong evidence to suggest that learners learn best when constructing their own knowledge. However, there is also a right time to clearly guide learners or simply give

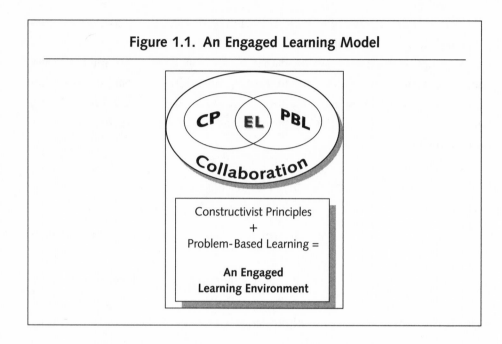

Figure 1.1. An Engaged Learning Model

them a critical piece of information to help them move forward" (p. 97). What is important is to value the desired outcome of the constructivist approach, which is that the acquisition of knowledge is centered on the learners and their interactions and not solely on a lecture-focused, instructor-centered approach.

ENGAGED LEARNING IN THE ONLINE ENVIRONMENT

While the history of education has been filled with instances in which students and teachers were focused on student-oriented learning, today's pedagogical evolution has added technology to the equation. New media offer a wealth of opportunities for interaction, yet many times are employed in a non-interactive mode that tends to focus on creating an online lecture. Lecture is effective for knowledge transmission, but if it is the primary strategy used in the online environment, the course becomes a digital correspondence course with potential problems of learner isolation and high dropout rate.

The involvement of the learner in the course, whether one calls it interaction, engagement, or building community, is critical if an online course is to be more than a lecture-oriented course in which interaction is primarily between the learner and the content or the learner and the instructor. Norris, Mason, and Lefrere (2003) emphasize that content may have been the primary focus of the past but the time is coming when interactivity will drive learning (p. x).

Engaged learning stimulates learners to actively participate in the learning situation, and thus gain the most knowledge from being a member of an online learning community. Activities can also serve as memory cues. On several occasions, students have reported remembering the lessons learned from an activity in order to trigger long-term memory relative to the recall of basic concepts. One learner stated that she could not answer a key midterm question until she thought about the associated activity, this caused her to remember the concepts that the activity presented, and the activated memory allowed her to organize and respond to the item in question.

Over the past decade, more knowledge about the value of engaged learning in an online environment has emerged (Palloff & Pratt, 1999, 2007; Collison, Elbaum, Haavind, & Tinker, 2000; Salmon, 2002; Woo & Reeves, 2007; Thorpe, 2008), but additional guidelines are needed to help instructors assist learners in evolving from their traditional role of receiving knowledge to a role that focuses on their generating knowledge for themselves and others.

Kearsley (2000) points out that "the most important role of the instructor in online classes is to ensure a high degree of interactivity and participation. This means designing and conducting learning activities that result in engagement with the subject matter and with fellow students" (p. 78).

Students cannot be passive knowledge-absorbers who rely on the instructor to feed information to them. In an online course, it is imperative that they be active knowledge-generators who assume responsibility for constructing and managing their own learning experience. In a learner-centered environment, the traditional instructor responsibilities such as generating resources and leading discussion shifts to the learners. Success in an online learning environment depends on the use of instructional strategies that support the shift in roles and the development of self-direction.

If the learners are to succeed in their new role as an active partner in knowledge generation, Weimer (2002) contends that the power inherent in a learning environment should be shared so that "faculty still make key decisions about learning, but they no longer make all decisions and not always without student input"

(Weimer, 2002, p. 28). The benefits of power sharing include energized learners who are motivated to stay with a course when the going gets rough. This also means that online power-sharing instructors may not have to struggle as much to keep learners engaged in the course. Online facilitators set the stage for power sharing to occur in the way they approach learners and provide feedback. When an online facilitator invites learners to be a part of the process, more often than not, learners rise to the occasion.

Leaders in the field of online education such as Draves (2000, 2009), Palloff and Pratt (1999, 2007), Moore and Kearsley (2004), and Simonson, Smaldino, Albright, and Zvacek (2008) all agree that learner interaction is the key to an effective online course. However, interaction and collaboration are not intuitive to many adult learners who grew up under the competitive model of education where learners had to outshine one another to be successful. Initially, a learner may be more comfortable in the perceived safe role of a passive student and will need guidance and the opportunity to exercise leadership and direction-setting in an online learning environment.

Engaged learning is a collaborative learning process in which the teacher and student are partners in constructing knowledge and answering essential questions. This strategic approach includes setting goals, establishing timelines, and creating and assessing authentic products. Key elements of engaged learning in an online environment include the following:

- Students establishing their own learning goals
- Students working together in groups
- Exploring appropriate resources to answer meaningful questions
- Tasks that are multidisciplinary and authentic, with connections to the real world
- Assessment that is ongoing and performance-based
- Products that are shared with an audience beyond the classroom so students are able to add value outside of the learning environment (Johnson, 1998)

The distance education pioneer Charles Wedemeyer (1981) asserted that learners must be highly self-motivated in order to be effective distance learners. While this is still true in today's online learning environment, the instructor also has the responsibility to support and promote a learner's internal motivations through external strategies. An engaged learning educational approach for instructors involves modeling, reflecting, actively involving the student, and developing a community of fellow learners.

Engaged learning requires a cognitive and affective learner connection with the methodology before it can occur. Gagne and Driscoll (1988) state that the following external learning conditions are needed to maximize the influence of engaged learning:

- The strategy is described or demonstrated.
- Numerous opportunities for communication and demonstration of the strategy are provided.
- An expectation of success associated with incorporating the strategy and attitude of engagement is presented.
- Informative feedback is provided as to the creativity and originality involved in learner actions as well as their successful performance by an engaged learner.

We would add the following items to this list:

- A safe student-centered learning environment is provided.
- Opportunities for self-assessment are provided.

Before a learner can effectively demonstrate the skills of an engaged learner, he or she must understand engaged learning and be amenable to adopting the strategy. Only then can a learner be expected to form a community with others in the online learning environment.

GUIDING LEARNERS TO ENGAGE ONLINE

The student's role as an engaged learner develops over time. Interaction and collaboration is not intuitive to many adult learners who have been educated in a predominantly lecture-based environment. Initially, a learner may be more comfortable in a passive student role and will need guidance and the opportunity to become more involved in an online learning environment. An online learner must quickly establish comfort with the technology, comfort with predominantly text-based communication, and comfort with a higher level of self-direction than in a traditional classroom. If this comfort level is not reached, the learner will walk away from the course in frustration.

In addition to these elements, learners have the additional uncertainty of having to quickly build trust and interdependence with others that they may never meet face to face. It becomes the instructor's responsibility to make sure that the learners find others in the learning environment with whom they can build a collaborative relationship. To do this, the online instructor must design course elements that encourage the growth of learners in these new relationships.

When courses first moved online, it seemed that more time was needed for an instructor to manage a successful course online than had been needed in the traditional classroom setting. The Phases of Engagement framework initially began as a desire to manage the level of online communication and focus learners and instructors on performing their new roles in the online environment.

This framework provides a means of developing appropriate activities and introducing them in an effective sequence. The framework includes introductory community-building exercises, which build trust and help a group learn how to work together. As learners gain more confidence and expertise, they can be guided to move through additional phases of engagement (see Table 1.1).

During Phase 1, the instructor and learner begin the course in the more traditional role of deliverer-receiver, with the instructor setting the initial tone of the course as being one in which he or she will be a guide. The students need to be informed that others in the community will be just as important as the instructor, if not more so at times. This tone can be set by an initial e-mail from the instructor or by having the first activity of the course be an icebreaker introduction that requires learners to learn about and interact with one another in a nonthreatening manner. There may be a tendency for new online instructors to rush through this initial phase, to get to what they may consider the heart of the course—the content. However, experienced online instructors have found that interaction is actually the essence of the course (Draves, 2000; Palloff & Pratt, 2007). The rest of the course will go much more smoothly if care is taken to promote the appropriate frame of mind in Phase 1 of the engagement process.

Table 1.1. Phases of Engagement

Phase	Learner Role	Instructor Role	Weeks	Process
1	Newcomer	Social negotiator	1–2	Instructor provides activities that are interactive and that help learners get to know one another. Instructor expresses expectations for engagement in the course, provides orientation to the course, and keeps learners on track. Examples: icebreakers, individual introductions, discussions concerning community issues such as Netiquette rules in a virtual lounge.
2	Cooperator	Structural engineer	3–4	Instructor forms dyads of learners and provides activities that require critical thinking, reflection, and sharing of ideas. *Examples:* Peer reviews, activity critiques.
3	Collaborator	Facilitator	5–6	Instructor provides activities that require small groups to collaborate, solve problems, reflect on experiences. *Examples:* content discussions, role playing, debates, jigsaws.
4	Initiator/ partner	Community member/ challenger	7–16	Activities are learner-designed or learner-led. Discussions begin to go not only where the instructor intends but also where the learners direct them to go. *Examples:* Group presentations and projects, learner-facilitated discussions.

After establishing an appropriate climate for engagement to occur in Phase 1, the instructor becomes a structural engineer who is responsible for organizing and facilitating the growth of the student as a cooperative participant. Based on information from the introductory activity, the instructor pairs students in working dyads. This approach minimizes the threat of communicating with a large group of unknown peers. Phase 2 may begin in a social tone similar to Phase 1, but it must then turn the learners toward more academic exchanges.

In Phase 3, the peer partners are combined into collaborative teams in which members support one another and are responsible for one another's learning. Our experience as online instructors is that it takes about four weeks for most learners to feel comfortable enough with technology-mediated communication and their cyberpeers to move into this phase. Is Phase 2 necessary, or can learner teams be formed immediately? Teams can be formed sooner under the following conditions:

- The size of the learning community is small (less than twenty members).
- There was a high degree of interaction in Phase 1 activities.
- Teaming is tightly structured with contracts and feedback rubrics provided by the instructor, or the majority of the learners are experienced online collaborators.

An instructor encourages learners to move to Phase 4 by introducing opportunities for individuals and teams to lead activities. In this phase, the instructor participates in the learning environment like any other member of the learning community, as another knowledge generator.

Movement through each of the initial phases is facilitated by the "activity architect," the instructor, who, through activities, provides increasing opportunities for learners to know and trust one another, with the goal of learners gradually being able to turn to a community as opposed to a single instructor for information and support. Not surprisingly, younger students may adapt more easily than older adults to meeting others online, but both groups may initially have difficulty shaking off the passivity of the lecture-based paradigm and turning to one another as sources of knowledge. Again, providing enough time to move through each of the phases is vital to effectively developing a fully engaged frame of mind in the learner.

APPROPRIATE ACTIVITIES FOR EACH PHASE

Designing and utilizing activities that are appropriate for the various engagement phases of specific learners can promote confidence and success and may even move a learner through the phases more quickly. Table 1.2 provides examples of phase-appropriate activities.

The Phase 1 example activity focuses on introducing peers to one another in a creative and fun manner. The Phase 2 example activity focuses on two peers working together, while the Phase 3 example demonstrates a reflective activity. The "Group Choice" example activity for Phase 4 exhibits how learners can be provided with the opportunity to lead an activity in the online community.

It is important to note that content-related engaged activities should not begin until a learner has completed Phase 1 and moved solidly into Phase 2. This is not to say that content-related activities cannot be done by a Phase 1 learner, but the most appropriate activities at this point would be individual rather than peer-related.

What if learners are experienced in the online environment? Can phases be skipped? While it may be possible to move more quickly through the phases, it is still recommended that the instructor use at least one activity from each phase in order to help learners become oriented to the course and become familiar with the new set of peers who will be working together in the online environment.

Part Two of this book provides additional examples of activities for each phase. Chapters Four and Five provide activities for Phase 1, Chapter Six for Phase 2, and Chapter Seven transitions the Phase 2 learner into Phase 3. Chapters Eight and Nine provide activities for Phase 3, and Chapter 10 for Phase 4.

SUMMARY

Engaged learning is not a new theoretical approach, but its application in an online environment requires special consideration in order to maximize learning. The challenge both educators and learners face is how to facilitate the

Table 1.2. Activity Examples for Each Phase of Engagement

Phase	Learner Role	Instructor Role	Activity Example	
1	Newcomer	Social negotiator	*Exercise Title:*	One Thing That Describes Me
			Task:	Student uses a symbol to describe himself or herself
			Objective:	To introduce a student's interests and background to others in the class
			Learner Instructions: Look around and find an object or a digital image that represents you, or your reasons for taking this course or even something about your research interests. Post a digital image of your chosen object—for example, a scanned image, digital picture, or a Web-linked image—on the discussion board. Explain why you chose the item. Your explanation of the posted object should include a brief description of your expectations of the course and/or the perspective you contribute to the learning community. After you enter your description, comment on the descriptions posted by at least two of your peers.	
2	Cooperator	Structural engineer	*Exercise Title:*	Pair Share
			Task:	Peers discuss reading questions
			Objective:	To process content
			Learner Instructions: After completing this week's reading, take a moment to answer the assigned questions (instructor provides content-related questions). Contact your assigned peer and discuss any questions you might have about the reading. What are your common perceptions? Where do you differ? Post your response in the discussion area.	

Table 1.2. *Continued*

Phase	Learner Role	Instructor Role	Activity Example	
3	Collaborator	Facilitator	*Exercise Title:*	Summary Words
			Task:	Student reflects on the course or unit so far
			Objective:	To provide feedback to the instructor and classmates on the shared experience
			Learner Instructions: Take a few minutes to reflect on your reactions to this week's class (or identified unit). What two or three word expressions come to mind? Enter a brief expression into the subject line of a discussion board thread. Post as many words or expressions as you can think of in five minutes. This is not the time to analyze your input; just key and post. Wait twenty-four hours, then review the responses of your peers. Choose one word or expression that speaks directly to you. Post a response to your peer and instructor explaining why this word has special meaning in defining the class experience for you.	
4	Initiator/ partner	Community member/ challenger	*Exercise Title:*	Group Choice
			Task:	Team designs class activity
			Objective:	To process content
			Learner Instructions: Your team will be required to develop and lead an activity that relates to the following objectives (instructor provides objectives). Be prepared to lead your activity during Week 8 of the course.	

transition between the mindset that was reinforced in the traditional lecture-based learning environment and the one required to be an engaged online community member.

Engaged learning does not simply happen. It requires "architectural engineering" by the instructor. Planning and utilizing activities that assist a learner in moving through the developmental phases of engaged learning ensures that learners are motivated and able to successfully interact and collaborate in an online learning environment and eventually engage in independent knowledge building.

Constructing Activities to Engage Online Learners

Designing Online Engagement

The learning community is the vehicle through which learning occurs online. Members depend on each other to achieve the learning outcomes for the course.

Palloff & Pratt, 2007, p. 40

An instructor can clearly detect when students are engaged in an effective classroom activity. Both energy and sound levels are higher, and students are reluctant to change to another task. The synergy between collaborative partners is exciting to observe as the discussion grows animated and connections are established. The big question is, how do you create this exhilarating learning environment when you lack verbal and visual cues? Salmon (2002) points out that the lack of these cues need not be viewed as detrimental, because it can mean freedom from the distraction of physical presence. "If the remoteness and lack of visual clues are handled appropriately they can increase the comfort level of e-moderators and participants alike" (p. 20).

Several decisions must be made in order to design an effective activity that will engage the learner appropriately. These include the following:

- Whether a classroom-based activity will be adapted for use online or an entirely new one designed
- How the needs of the learner will be met
- What communication tool will be the most effective for the activity

ADAPTING CLASSROOM-BASED ACTIVITIES

As instructional technology tools were developing, the level of technology sometimes drove the learning experience. However, it is the learning outcome that must be the focus of the activity, not the technological tool used to implement the activity. Thus, designing online activities is very similar to designing classroom-based activities.

To determine whether a classroom-based activity is adaptable to the online environment, the activity must first be examined to see that it meets the learning outcomes of the online course. Often a classroom-based course is redesigned before it is put online, and learning outcomes or objectives are modified. Every activity should be scrutinized to determine whether it matches a learning objective. An activity that does not contribute to a learning outcome only adds confusion to the course and risks learner dissatisfaction at having to do an unnecessary activity.

In an engaged learning environment, the majority of learning outcomes should fall into the application, analysis, synthesis, or evaluation levels of thinking as described in Bloom's taxonomy (Bloom, 1956). Each activity to be used for online engaged learning should be analyzed to determine which level of thinking it requires and to ensure that there is a mix of activities for varying levels of thinking.

The next element to consider is how appropriate the activity is for use in an engaged learning environment. Analyze how this activity will contribute to engaged learning, using the following questions:

- Will the activity help learners use the online tools?
- Does it assist in the social process needed to establish community?
- What type of interaction or collaboration with peers occurs?
- Is reflection required?
- Will a particular problem be resolved?

Also consider which phase of engagement the activity could be classified under and whether the activity is placed appropriately in the sequence of the course. For example, a Phase 4 student-led discussion activity should not occur in the first few weeks of a course, because the learning community will not have been adequately prepared for it. To introduce it prematurely would guarantee its failure. An instructor-facilitated discussion would be a more appropriate activity.

Smith and Ragan (1999) caution against the limited perspective that learner enthusiasm and engagement always equates with learning taking place. Activities that lack an instructional goal and purpose will fail to create a deeper level of community and knowledge acquisition even if they are fun and interactive. Beware of what Smith and Ragan term the "activity for activity's sake" approach (1999, p. 17). Sequencing and using activities as described in the four-phase approach will help you avoid meaningless activities.

There are some activities that can be easily converted from face-to-face to online interactions; brainstorming is one of the most obvious. To quickly "shout out" phrases in an online situation, use the subject line of a threaded discussion to enter the thought. This allows everyone to quickly read the idea without having to open the document.

Small-group interactions can be facilitated in an assigned discussion or chat area for each group, with the instructor going from group to group and interjecting comments, as is done in a face-to-face classroom. Group reporting can be assigned to one individual, who may provide a summary for a synchronous class discussion or in an asynchronous discussion area.

New activities will still be needed in addition to those converted from a classroom-based environment. At the very minimum, activities to help learners use the online tools and to promote the social development of the online community will need to be designed. The questions outlined in this section should also be considered when planning these new activities.

When adapting in-class activities to a hybrid or blended learning environment in which some classroom face-to-face contact is combined with an online component, consider those activities that would benefit from being introduced in the classroom setting and then enhanced through further online discussion. For example, if a class meets every third week with the interim two weeks designed for online interaction, introduce the topic in the classroom and then use the online interaction time to expand knowledge development and content processing. Another approach is to begin an online dialogue or task in preparation for a face-to-face classroom discussion. This approach may prove useful for assignments that focus on sensitive areas or would benefit from allowing for in-depth student reflection time and comment prior to an instructor-facilitated class discussion.

MEETING THE NEEDS OF ONLINE LEARNERS

The lives of online learners are complicated, with numerous distractions and motivational challenges. "Most of our students today are older, are working, and need more flexible schedules" (Palloff & Pratt, 2001, p. 109). They face challenges such as family needs, business travel, and health issues. The learning process can be interrupted by births, weddings, illnesses, deaths, unexpected career changes, international business meetings, and long-overdue vacations. There will be technological glitches as well, but the personal hurdles will far outweigh the technological ones.

For many participants, their first few experiences in an online learning community can be overwhelming. The key to creating a positive experience is to identify the students' needs and then incorporate activities that address their various learning styles, life experiences, and expectations. For an online facilitator, this means getting to know the learner as soon as possible through the use of profiles and introductory activities that provide insight into who the learner is not only academically but professionally and personally. The facilitator can then begin to draw on the experiences of those in the course and empower course members to capitalize on what they know. Adult learners bring a diverse set of experiences and perspectives with them to the learning environment. They do not learn in a vacuum but in the rich context of the life they have lived and are currently living. In a learner-centered environment, those experiences are honored and woven into the academic experience through discussion and activities that provide opportunities for learners to lead. It also means that a facilitator stands ready to adjust activities as the needs of the community dictate. For example, discussion questions can be modified or added based on the diversity of the learning community. Project topics can be chosen by the learners rather than assigned by the instructor.

Another consideration is the changing demographics of our students. American society presently consists of more adults than youth with an increasing ethnic and cultural diversity which necessitates that "certain learning activities are learner-activated and others are society-initiated in response to the changing demographics" (Merriam, Caffarella, & Baumgartner, 2007, p. 7). Generational differences can have a significant impact on how learners interact. Technology has affected not only how we teach but how our students learn. "For today's students, the classroom is the world, and the information students have available at the flip of a switch is infinite" (Cross, 2007, p. 55). Today's online classroom provides evidence that there is no "typical" student.

One fundamental aspect of meeting the needs of online learners is allowing adequate time for an activity to be accomplished. Online communication takes longer than classroom communication in most cases. Therefore, more time must be allowed in the course plan for activities requiring online interaction among learners than might be provided in the course plan of a face-to-face class. Discussion activities need a minimum of a week to develop. If more than one discussion is conducted at a time, learners should be allowed to choose the topics that they will participate in discussing. Teams need to begin planning their projects at least six weeks before they are due. Too many activities in a week will overwhelm learners. Remember that the depth of thought is likely to be greater in a reflective online discussion than in a reactive classroom-based discussion. Fewer activities, rather than more, will improve the quality of knowledge generation.

CHOOSING AN EFFECTIVE COMMUNICATION TOOL

While the technology should not be the primary focus when planning an activity, choosing the most effective means of conducting the activity will be an important contributor to its success. For example, a reflective activity that is conducted using a synchronous chat may turn into a reactive exercise in which learners are typing too quickly to think as deeply as they might in an asynchronous discussion.

Table 2.1 lists the characteristics of some tools that are commonly available for activities. For instance, announcements, course documents, and CD-ROMs are broadcast tools, which provide one-way communication from the initiator to the receiver. Conversely, interactive tools, such as discussion boards, chat rooms, Skype, a group wiki, virtual worlds, and e-mail, allow a communication exchange to occur. Communication can be public or private. For example, an announcement is a public communication tool, while an e-mail message is a more private form of communication.

Social networking is an activity that is used by many of our students. Facebook and Twitter are social tools that have become communication choices for many learners. Using social networking tools to engage students in course discussions can be beneficial. Clear boundaries can be set by creating a Facebook site that is limited to just class members and course tasks. The sharing of professional learning networks (PLNs) can also allow students to provide important links and resources relative to class content as they build their own knowledge bases.

The technology tools available to an online community include some that are not used online. Telephones and fax machines can be used along with online tools. For example, in one of our classes, a student arranged a conference call for the class to participate in a team-led presentation. One team member provided the lecture over the phone while another managed the accompanying PowerPoint slides and another typed the presentation transcript in the course chat room. This now also can be done with various web conferencing tools such as Elluminate, Adobe Acrobat Connect, and WebEx.

The question of whether to use a synchronous or asynchronous communication tool is a difficult one. Synchronous, or real-time communication occurs at the same time for all participants. Asynchronous communication occurs at varying times. In our fast-paced world, many of us feel the pressure to have instant answers to our communications. Many educators favor synchronous interaction because they are influenced by the classroom paradigm. Often instructors attempt to replicate a face-to-face classroom in the online environment because it is difficult to imagine how an activity works when learners are not participating at the same time, in the same space.

Table 2.1. Characteristics of Online Communication Tools

Communication Tool	Broadcast (B)/ Interactive (I)	Public/ Private	Online/ Offline	Synchronous (S)/ Asynchronous (A)	• One-to-One (O) • One-to-Small Group (S) • One-to-Large Group (L)	Group Interaction (Many-to-Many) (M)
Study guide/ CD-ROM	B	Public	Offline	A	L	
Announcements	B	Public	Online	A	L	
Course documents (video/audio/ text files)	B	Public	Online	A	L	
Student pages	B	Public	Online	A	L	
E-mail	I	Private	Online	A	O, S, L	
Discussion board	I	Public	Online	A	S, L	M
Chat	I	Public	Online	S	O, S, L*	
Skype****	I	Public	Online	S	O, S	
Group wiki	I	Public	Online	A	S, L	
Blog	I	Public	Online	A	S, L	
Virtual worlds (ex. Second Life)	I	Public	Online	S	O, S, L	M (group presentations)*

Continued

Table 2.1. Continued

Communication Tool	Broadcast (B)/ Interactive (I)	Public/ Private	Online/ Offline	Synchronous (S)/ Asynchronous (A)	• One-to-One (O) • One-to-Small Group (S) • One-to-Large Group (L)	Group Interaction (Many-to-Many) (M)
Webcasting (ex. Adobe Connect)	I	Public	Online	S	S, L	
Instant messaging	I	Private	Online	S	O, S	
Assignment drop box	I	Private	Online	A	O	
Group (to group) discussion area	I	Private	Online	A, S**	O, S	
Phone	I	Private	Offline	S	O, S	
Fax	B, (I)****	Private	Offline	A	O	
Overnight mail	B	Private	Offline	A	O	

*Break larger groups into smaller groups to increase interaction and decrease chaos

**Assumes existence of discussion board and chat capabilities within the group area

***Dependent on the speed of response

****Skype is one example of Voice over Internet Protocol (VoIP) which allows telephone-like communication via the Internet

There are some situations in which synchronous activities are the most effective choice, such as when conducting team meetings or when building group consensus. But synchronous activities entail many challenges. Trying to coordinate a meeting time is often difficult. Another consideration is the structure of the discussion. Several topics may become active at the same time, causing discussions to become fragmented. Also, the fastest typist tends to be the loudest voice. To avoid these problems, the facilitator can limit the discussion to one topic at a time and ensure that all participants have posted comments before a second topic is introduced. Keeping the number of participants small allows easier tracking when using this approach.

Another major frustration for learners involved in a synchronous activity occurs when the technology fails. When learners are unable to log in to a scheduled chat session, they feel they have missed class and the sole opportunity to participate through no fault of their own. Logs of the synchronous discussions are imperative in order to minimize this de-motivating aspect of synchronous communication. It is also important to provide instructions in advance for an alternate class activity in case the synchronous session is interrupted due to network problems.

Despite the fact that it does not happen within a shared time period, asynchronous communication has many benefits. It allows for reflective time prior to response. The depth of thought in asynchronous activities is usually greater than in synchronous activities, unless significant preparation is required before chat sessions. Asynchronous activities also allow the instructor and learners to communicate at their most productive time of the day, when thoughts are clearest and minds freshest. Learners can choose to interact during their individual "teachable moments." Unlike synchronous activities, asynchronous activities allow each voice to be heard, whether in a small or large group, helping learners feel that they are part of a learning community and increasing their motivation to interact.

One danger of asynchronous communication is its open-endedness. There must be a distinct beginning and end to asynchronous activities in order to minimize information overload and subsequent learner frustration. When used appropriately, the opportunity for reflective thought and communication in an asynchronous activity can produce far greater depth of learning than typically occurs in a synchronous activity.

Choose communication tools based on the nature of the activity. Use synchronous communication for quick exchanges of thought. Consider mixing synchronous and asynchronous activities. For example, group discussions could be conducted asynchronously, but team meetings could be conducted synchronously.

The final consideration when choosing a communication tool for an online engaged learning activity is whether communication needs to be one-to-one, as in peer reviews; one-to–small group, as might occur in a team meeting; one-to–large group, as in instructor-to-class announcements; or many-to-many, as might occur between groups. For example, one-to-one communications can be served by all the interactive tools listed in Table 2.1, while one-to–small group communications are best served by tools such as e-mail or discussion in the group area of a course management system.

SUMMARY

A student's learning process is enhanced through careful activity preparation on the part of the instructor or course designer. The goal is to create activities that will engage and challenge learners while expanding their personal connections to their existing knowledge.

When moving an activity from the classroom to an online learning environment, the instructor must consider whether the activity will result in appropriate learning outcomes, what level of thinking it promotes, whether it will engage the learning community, and what communication tools should be used. Awareness of students' varied learning styles and needs also influences the design of effective engaged learning activities for the online environment.

If a classroom-based activity cannot be converted for use in an online learning environment, a new activity must be developed with the learning outcomes, learners' needs, and communication tool selection in mind. At minimum, new activities will be needed in the online environment to help learners use the new online communication tools and to help the community develop its social interactions.

Measuring Online Engaged Learning

*Assessment of interaction and collaboration is challenging,
and it cannot represent a true picture of individual knowledge
and skills acquired unless the activities and teams have been
planned and structured in an effective manner.*

Oosterhoff, Conrad, & Ely, 2008, p. 202

The primary indicators of engagement in an online learning environment are the amount of interaction between students and the quality of that interaction. A high volume of meaningful communication, a deeper level of understanding, and the application of knowledge to real-life situations all combine to engage the students and instructor in the learning situation. The posting of an "aha" moment at 3 A.M. or the metamorphosis of discussion and understanding into complex ideas are all signs that the course is on the path of engaged learning.

ANALYZING THE QUALITY OF CRITICAL THINKING

As in any course, effective assessment of engaged learning must be built into the very structure of the course. Dick, Carey, and Carey (2009) recommend that assessments be determined directly after the desired learning outcomes have been defined and before the bulk of the course activities are constructed. This process does not differ in an online engaged learning environment. What does differ is the assessment strategy.

In an engaged learning environment, learners are required to perform at the higher levels of thinking in Bloom's taxonomy, which are application, analysis, synthesis, and evaluation (Bloom, 1956). Traditional exams with multiple-choice questions are adequate for the knowledge and comprehension levels of Bloom's taxonomy but cannot accurately measure the depth of critical thinking and reflection that occurs in an engaged learning environment. Evaluation of critical thinking and reflection requires assessment methods that encourage individual expression, perhaps through answering open-ended questions or completing a culminating project. The instructor may intersperse self-assessment activities throughout the course or use nongraded activities that allow learners to explore ideas in a nonthreatening environment.

Large online class enrollments leave many instructors with limited evaluation choices, which may result in the use of standard testing methodologies in order to provide timely feedback. However, in an engaged learning environment, alternative means of assessment that are incorporated throughout the course should be used in concert with traditional exams whenever possible in order to evaluate higher levels of thinking. For example, having learners demonstrate their understanding through a group project or paper whose topic they define requires more than rote learning and maximizes the level of thinking promoted in an engaged learning environment.

The assessment strategies that are most effective in an engaged learning environment—such as projects, papers, discussion postings, and student-led discussions—also require additional tools; discussion analysis tools, rubrics, team assessments, and reflective self-assessments can help to effectively measure individual performance in an engaged learning environment.

When considering the assessment of critical thinking in discussion, papers, and projects, an instructor must consider how it will be demonstrated. Palloff and Pratt (2003) list the following attributes of critical thinking, which could be used in the development of a rubric for discussions, projects, and papers:

- Clarity of ideas and expression
- Consistency of behavior and thinking
- Openness to learning
- Evaluation of material
- Communication
- Specificity of feedback
- Accessibility for discussion
- Flexibility
- Risk-taking

DISCUSSION ANALYSIS TOOLS

The greatest challenge in assessing an online engaged activity is determining the quality of thought expressed. Online instructors often feel as if they must read every discussion posting in order to adequately evaluate each learner's depth of critical thinking. New software tools are emerging that assist with this task so that an instructor doesn't have to read everything. One such tool is the Discussion Analysis Tool, also known as ForumManager, which evaluates patterns in online interactions (Jeong, 2003).

The analysis results produced by ForumManager include the average number of discussion entries per participant, the level of interactivity, richness of the discussion, and depth of the discussion. These assessment data can be used as one factor in formulating a grade or to prompt additional interactions and provide feedback that encourages deeper critical thinking in online discussions.

RUBRICS

A rubric defines the performance levels for each gradable activity element. The creation of activity rubrics can be time-consuming but is well worth the effort, because both the learner and teacher expectations are better met when evaluation criteria are provided at the time a task is assigned. A rubric clearly specifies the expectations for the activity and the effort required by the student to achieve a desired score.

To construct a rubric, list each key element of the activity, then define the various levels of effort and determine the grading points for each level. If an activity requires multiple types of effort, a rubric for each effort type must be constructed. The examples in Tables 3.1 through 3.3 are based on an activity in Chapter Nine, entitled Group Problem-Based Learning Activity, that was developed by Charleen Worsham of Kilgore College in Texas. The goals of the project are to simulate a real-world situation and to provide an experience for group problem-based learning. Each team member acts as a computer support expert, and each team must prepare hardware, software, operating system, and peripheral device specifications for new employees. For this activity, two rubrics were constructed—one for the specifications produced by the team and one for the level of required teamwork. In addition, a reflective self-assessment was used.

TEAM ASSESSMENTS

In an engaged learning environment, peers often have the best perspective on whether their teammates are providing valuable contributions to the learning community. Therefore, learning environments that encourage collaborative activities should incorporate peer evaluations in the assessment process.

A major drawback of this type of assessment is that students are often reluctant to criticize someone else's efforts. The key to effective peer feedback is that it be constructive and encourage improvement. One recommended approach is to identify how it might be improved or changed the next time as opposed to only pointing out its deficiencies. Another way to have course participants evaluate one another's contributions in a group effort is to use a rubric such as the one in Table 3.2 or the form developed by Mary Herring at the University of Northern Iowa, shown in Exhibit 3.1.

By including team assessments as part of the project grade, the instructor can emphasize the importance of collaboration. If there are discrepancies in team members' assessments, the instructor may wish to phone or e-mail to see why one member viewed the experience or team performance in a different light than

Table 3.1. Example of a Project Rubric

Rubric Used to Evaluate Project for Group Problem-Based Learning Activity (see Chapter Nine)

The following scoring rubric will be used to evaluate your completed project on each of the criteria listed, and points will be awarded as indicated. Each student and the instructor will score each group project.

Points

Criteria	0	2	4	6
Overall Computer Specifications	The specifications show no evidence of analysis.	The specifications show evidence that the group reached conclusions not based on data analysis, or the specifications show valid conclusions but lack evidence of analysis.	The specifications show evidence that the group reached valid conclusions based on data analysis but displayed the results of the analysis in inappropriate formats.	The specifications show evidence that the group reached valid conclusions based on data analysis and displayed the results of the analysis in appropriate formats.
Coverage of System Unit Components				
Coverage of Application Software				
Coverage of Input Devices				
Coverage of Output Devices				
Coverage of Storage Devices				
Coverage of Operating System and Utility Programs				

Continued

Table 3.1. Continued

Criteria	Points			
	0	2	4	6
Appropriateness of Specifications to End-User Needs	Proposed specifications do not fit with end-user needs.	Proposed specifications loosely fit with end-user needs.	Proposed specifications fit somewhat with end-user needs.	Proposed specifications fit tightly with end-user needs.
Budget and Cost Justification	Proposed specifications do not include budget information.	Budget information provided is incomplete or lacks justification.	Budget information provided is complete, but nonstandard items are not adequately justified.	Budget information is complete, and nonstandard items are justified.
Individual Contribution to Group Project	Report missing evidence of contribution.	Contribution document but not justified.	Contribution evident but did not impact final project.	Contribution well stated and effective.
Writing Clarity	Report contains misspelled words, improper punctuation, and bad grammar. Report has no apparent structure.	Writing is generally clear, and report is generally easy to follow.	Writing is clear and report is easy to follow, but meaning is sometimes hidden.	Writing is clear and succinct. Reader can easily identify what writers are trying to express. Grammar and punctuation are correct.

Table 3.2. Example of a Team Rubric

Rubric to Evaluate Team Participation for Group Problem-Based Learning Activity (see Chapter Nine)

Score yourselves and each of your group members, based on the following criteria:

Points

Criteria	0	2	3	4
Cooperation	Did not listen to and did not value the opinion of others	Listened to but did not value the opinion of others, or valued the opinions of others but did not listen to them	Actively listened to but it was not evident that he or she valued the opinion of others	Actively listened to and valued the opinions of others
Contribution	Did not contribute to the completion of the project	Contributed to the project, but work was inferior or inadequate	Contributed to the completion of the project with adequate work	Contributed to the completion of the project and submitted high-quality work
Participation	Did not participate in the group	Occasionally participated in the group	Often participated in the group	Consistently participated in the group

Table 3.3. Example of a Self-Assessment Activity

Share your reflections on the assignment as follows:

Question	Reflective Thoughts
What I learned about buying a computer . . .	
What I learned about working with others in an online group . . .	
The time and effort required to complete this assignment compared to what I learned was . . .	
What I learned that I can transfer into my work or personal life included . . .	

the other members. Open discussions between students and the instructor to explain differences usually result in a new understanding of expectations and can be an opportunity to improve conflict resolution skills.

One of the common concerns voiced by students is grading equity for group projects. One way to fairly assess a collaborative project is to identify the components on the rubric that represent individual contributions. These elements may include documentation on the individual's involvement, new skills obtained, new insights, and a reflection on the process. Some instructors have developed rubrics that reflect almost half of the final project grade to be targeted at an individual's contribution.

REFLECTIVE SELF-ASSESSMENTS

Reflection and self-assessment are important components for empowerment in any learner-focused environment. Journaling, in which learners produce documents representing their thoughts throughout an activity, is one of the primary tools for tracking both formative and summative self-assessment. One important concept is considering "transformative learning" as a function of reflection (Mezirow, 1991). How the newly acquired knowledge will change the learner's

Exhibit 3.1. Example of a Peer Evaluation Form

Peer Evaluation (15 points)

Evaluator Name: _____

Module Number: _____

List each team member, and rate them on a scale from 1 to 3 in each of the areas listed.

3 = Above average

2 = Average

1 = Below average

Quality (3 points): Completed all assignments at the level of quality expected by the group

Responsibility (3 points): Completed all assignments in a timely manner

Teamwork (3 points): Worked well with other team members

Contribution (3 points): Contributed to the group in an equitable fashion

Attitude (3 points): Projected positive attitude throughout module

Member Name	Quality	Responsibility	Teamwork	Contribution	Attitude

Additional comments:

Exhibit 3.2. Example of a Reflective Diary Activity

Instructions:

This diary is a *record of your reflections* about your own experiences, attitudes, opinions, and feelings in relation to the material and within the context of leadership. You should *make entries several times each week* as your thoughts develop about leadership, forever striving to develop your personal theory of information leadership. Keep in mind the theme of the class: Learning to Lead from Where You Are. Entries must be dated; for example, "Week 2, Sept. 4, 2002."

Random journal checks will be done throughout the semester. You should be prepared to *submit a current, digital copy upon request.* Thus, you would submit a diary with entries for Weeks 2–5 if we ask you to submit in Week 6. Generally, we will make an announcement four to six days prior to the due date.

Objective: To assist students in developing their personal theory-in-use of information leadership.

Task:

- Begin your diary in Week 2.

- Make at least one entry each week. You should have two to three pages per week.

- Date your entries.

- Write in an essay format, revealing your thoughts about how the material we're studying relates to your life in the context of leadership.

- Strive throughout the semester to develop and elucidate your personal theory of information leadership. You should revise your definition of information leadership throughout the semester based on classroom experiences, readings, and reflection.

The Personal Reflection Questions at the end of each chapter of the textbook may help you in relating the material to your own experiences, attitudes, opinions, and feelings; however, don't just answer the questions. This is your diary. It must reflect your thoughts.

Format: Essay, two to three pages per week, double-spaced, 12-point font, one-inch margins, typed.

Grade: Grading will consider your application of concepts to personal experience and/or knowledge. Grading will include our assessment of the depth of your thought. Each submission grade will be accumulated to determine the Reflective Diary grade for the semester.

understandings and actions is key to effective reflection. Requiring students to provide reflective journal entries for instructor review encourages participants to make sense of the online process and their position within the learning community. Exhibit 3.2 shows a reflective journal assignment that was developed by Robert F. Brooks and Rita-Marie Conrad at Florida State University.

SUMMARY

Assessment in an engaged learning environment should focus on whether the stated objectives of the course have been met and whether the students have been engaged in the learning process. Engaged learning requires a higher level of thinking; therefore, assessment should consist of more than traditional exams whenever possible. Activity rubrics, team assessment, and reflective self-assessment can be used to more effectively assess performance in an online engaged learning environment. In addition, software such as ForumManager can be used to analyze the depth of thought expressed through online communication.

CHAPTER
4

Learning to Use Online Tools

For the instructor of an online course, one of the biggest challenges is making sure that all participants have the necessary skill level with the communication tools that will be used during the course. Several activities can be used to increase the comfort level of all participants.

One of the initial steps in course development is determining which tools will be used in the course. Once the instructor determines the course requirements, the skill level of the students needs to be determined. A skills survey form is included as a suggested way of assessing the participants' previous experiences and current concerns. The instructor must be flexible enough to add skill-building activities when necessary. Sometimes skill-building activities need to be added for selected individuals after their skill levels are determined at the initial session.

BUILDING STUDENTS' SKILLS IN USING THE NECESSARY TOOLS

To avoid unnecessary frustration, we recommend that students be comfortable with a tool prior to its use in a graded assignment. Offering a nongraded assignment on Internet searching during a session prior to the due date of an actual graded search will eliminate the panic that is experienced by many students when faced with a graded assignment that requires the use of a new tool or process. For example, when using an assignment drop box, the instructor can assign a noncritical task as the first homework task.

In addition to providing opportunities for students to acquire the necessary skills, an instructor can establish an informal mentoring system by matching a more technologically skilled student with one with more limited experience. By having the two learners ask each other questions they have about an assignment, they learn from each other as opposed to relying on the expertise of the instructor. When the less experienced student has the answer to a peer's question, it offers an incredible opportunity for empowerment for that student. The saying "we learn best when we teach" applies very well to this situation. Not only does this approach free up the instructor's time, but it offers an opportunity for the participants to learn facilitation skills.

Once skills have been acquired, tracking students' use of the technology is essential. Whenever students rely on using technology to meet a course requirement, the excuses for nonsubmittal of an assignment such as "the dog ate my homework" or multiple deaths of the same grandmother in one semester have been replaced with more imaginative alternatives such as crashing hard drives, viruses, and unsaved lost files. One way for technology-assisted instructors to verify that due dates have been met is by using a drop box or tracking the time stamps on electronic transmissions. In the event of a technology failure, the learner should notify the instructor immediately to negotiate another means of assignment submittal. Students should also be advised to keep multiple copies of an assignment.

The best way for students to learn to use the online course tools is to actually use them. The more opportunities that are made available to students to increase their comfort level with course tools, the sooner the actual course content can be introduced.

An additional consideration is the individual learning style of the student and her or his comfort with the online environment. The Are You Ready for Learning Online? activity questions students to see if they are ready to make the transition from the familiarity of the classroom to the online environment. A low score might not necessarily exclude someone from online participation but will provide an indication of the learner's readiness for a successful experience.

Table 4.1. Skill-Building Activities to Try

Activity	Asynchronous	Synchronous
Are You Ready for Learning Online?	✓	
Skills Survey (student assessment)	✓	
Drag and Drop	✓	
Library Search (online library search)	✓	
I Can Find That (Boolean search techniques)	✓	
Scavenger Hunt (Internet search)	✓	
Syllabus Quiz	✓	

Are You Ready for Learning Online?

Name: _____

Number where you fall on the scale:
I agree = 10 . . . Sometimes = 5 . . . Not ever = 1
10 means that you agree with the statement, and 1 means that you do not agree at all.

_____

_____ *Number*

I'm open minded about sharing life, work, and
educational experiences as part of the learning process.

I'm able to communicate through writing.

I'm self-motivated and self-disciplined.

I'm willing to speak up if problems arise.

I'm willing and able to commit to 4 to 15 hours per
week per course.

I'm able to meet the minimum requirements for the
program.

I accept critical thinking and decision making as part of
the learning process.

I have practically unlimited access to a computer and
the Internet.

I'm able to think ideas through before responding

I feel that high-quality learning can take place without
going to a traditional classroom.

Total Score: _____

Additional comments:
If you score 100–75, you are probably ready for an online program or course.
If you score 40–74, you may need to work a bit harder to be successful online.
If you score below 39, online may not be for you at this point in your life.
Activity adapted from: Illinois Online Network. (2003). What makes a successful online student? Available at http://www.ion.uillinois.edu/resources/tutorials/pedagogy/studentprofile.asp.

Skills Survey

Name:

	Yes	No	Comments

1. I've participated in other online courses.
2. I feel comfortable using e-mail.
3. I have used an assignment drop box.
4. I can attach files to e-mail: text files, audio files, and digital images.
5. I feel comfortable using a discussion board, group area, wiki, or chat room.
6. I have participated in a threaded discussion.
7. I can effectively search for items on the Internet.
8. I feel comfortable using Boolean logic (and, or, +, −, and so on) when searching the Internet.
9. I have participated in online collaborations such as team projects or presentations.
10. I have used course management software (for example, Blackboard©, WebCT©, eCollege).

Previous online courses:

Additional comments:

Authors' Note

You are encouraged to modify this list to include the type of technology skills or tools that will be needed in a particular course. The students' abilities to use Skype, virtual environments (i.e., Second Life), and Web 2.0 tools (i.e., Google Docs) might all be useful to know prior to class assignments. We are living in a rapidly changing techie world and need to know what our students use and their skill levels.

Drag and Drop

Task: A game on how to enhance one's learning space

Objective: To help learners determine what might be helpful in a physical environment when learning online

Author: William Draves, President, Learning Resources Network (LERN), draves@lern.org

Method: Asynchronous

Instructions

Your physical environment is important when you learn online. Some things help your online learning; others hinder it.

1. Go to http://www.lern.org/applications/draganddrop/draganddrop.htm. The object of the game is to place the right objects in your online learning space (the "IN" box) and to place the objects that don't belong in the "OUT" box.

2. Click on the object and drag (move) it to one of the boxes. If you drag an object into the wrong box, it will snap back to its original location. For an explanation of each pair of objects, click on Notes.

3. When you are done, click on Submit.

Activity Author's Note

When a person does a drag-and-drop activity, the physical exercise in cyberspace increases memory, retention, and learning compared with a less physical exercise such as taking a multiple-choice test. Thus, the drag-and-drop activity has an underlying valid learning principle. I thank eighth-grader Tristan Wiley for his assistance in the development of this activity.

Library Search

Task:	Skills activity for learning how to do on-line library searches
Objective:	To help students learn online library searching
Author:	Kathleen R. Crane, MSN, RN, BC, Assistant Professor/Clinical, School of Nursing, The University of Texas Health Science Center at San Antonio, crane@uthscsa.edu
Method:	Asynchronous

Instructions

This assignment requires you to do an online library search for one article related to a topic covered in this course. You must submit the article and a one-page synopsis to your clinical instructor via e-mail. (It's not acceptable unless it's an electronic submission.)

Activity Author's Note

In our nursing program, we have many students who are new to using computers; many still don't have e-mail at home. As at many schools, students at the Health Science Center are given an e-mail account when they register. We include this library search assignment in our course, "Professional Nursing: Health Promotion." Based on suggestions and recommendations from previous students, this is now part of a graded activity worth 5 percent of the course grade.

For many students, when they complete this exercise, it is the first time they have used the online library facility and their e-mail. Most of them say, "That wasn't as hard as I thought it would be!"

Authors' Note

An extension of this activity would be to have all articles posted to the course website for student sharing. Future discussion questions and activities can be created around the submitted articles. Another approach would be to have students identify the top five articles that they found the most useful and explain why.

I Can Find That

Task:	Skills activity for learning Boolean search techniques
Objective:	To provide students with practice in using Boolean search techniques
Author:	J. Ana Donaldson, Ed.D., Walden University, ana.donaldson@waldenu.edu
Method:	Asynchronous

Instructions

You will be e-mailed a topic to search for on the Internet. You will have one week to submit your completed assignment. The trick of this task is to go from the largest number of Internet "hits" to the minimum number in the fewest number of searches by using the Boolean search techniques that we have discussed. Try several different browsers to determine which is the most effective for your particular search parameters.

You are to report only on the one that narrowed the topic to the fewest number of searches. Your final report should contain the following items:

- Search topic
- Browser name
- Initial Boolean search statement and number of "hits"
- Each of the subsequent Boolean statements and number of "hits"
- The final URL that best meets your search specifications
- Total number of searches performed

Good luck and think creatively!

Activity Author's Note

This activity is based on the old game show claim, "I can name that tune in five notes or less." It is important to provide students with basic information on how to do Boolean searches (and, or, +, and so on) prior to assigning this activity.

Author's Note:

I have used this activity for many years. I ask students to determine the color of Ben Franklin's eyes. However, the last time I used this activity I changed the search to Betsy Ross' eye color. I learned my lesson about providing clear instructions when a student from Taiwan had a different answer than the rest of the class. She had found the eye color for a Betsy Ross who was living in New Jersey!

Scavenger Hunt

Task:	Skills activity to help students learn to navigate on the Internet
Objective:	To increase students' ability to navigate on the Internet
Author:	Sarah Lelgarde Swart, Instructional Design Studio Director of Instructional Technology, University of Detroit-Mercy, swartsa@udmercy.edu
Method:	Asynchronous

Instructions

You will be provided a list of ten questions to answer. Use your search skills on the Internet to find the correct answers. E-mail both your answers and the associated URL to your instructor. Bonus points will be awarded to the top three students, based on correctness and speed of completion.

Activity Author's Note

After teaching some knowledge management and search skills such as Boolean logic, assign your students a ten-question scavenger hunt, asking them to give you the site where they found the answer.

Doing a browser search on the term "scavenger hunt" will produce some useful sites for creating your ten-question list or obtaining a ready-made tool.

Authors' Note

One effective way to use this activity is as a review prior to a course quiz on new content material. Not letting students know in advance that the questions will appear on the quiz is one way of reinforcing the value of successful searching techniques.

Syllabus Quiz

Task:	Introductory exercise for the beginning of a course
Objective:	To provide an opportunity for students to demonstrate their understanding of the course's orientation documents
Author:	Martha Kendall, Instructional Technologies, Monroe Community College, Rochester, NY, mkendall@monroecc.edu
Method:	Asynchronous

Instructions

You are expected to be familiar with the course syllabus, assignment due dates, and course orientation materials. The instructor will e-mail you a multiple-choice quiz. You will have one week to post your responses to the instructor as an attachment in .RTF file format. You will earn extra points if you post your response at least seventy-two hours before the due date.

Activity Author's Note

Assign students to read the orientation documents, which include the course syllabus and assignment due dates. Using a multiple-choice quiz, test them on the syllabus and critical due dates or technical elements of the course (for example, all written assignments must be received as attachments). All responses must be in .RTF file format. If students are slow to submit written assignments, add a new document to the course. In the document, announce that anyone who submits a written assignment at least seventy-two hours before the due date will get additional points.

Authors' Note

Since this is often the first task for the students in a class, it is recommended that it not be graded. Many learning management systems (i.e., Blackboard) have now simplified this task by including online testing within the course.

Activities to Engage
Online Learners

Online Icebreakers

The purpose of an icebreaker activity is to establish the presence of individuals and open the lines of communication for the learning community in a nonthreatening manner. Knowles (1980) stated that setting up an appropriate learning climate is key to establishing a successful learning experience. He described this climate as one "which causes adults to feel accepted, respected, and supported" with in "an atmosphere which is friendly and informal" (p. 47). An icebreaker sets the tone for such a learning environment.

Meyer (2002) summarized several research studies, all of which point to the positive impact on learning and satisfaction of "social presence" or "the degree to which a person is perceived as real in an online conversation" (p. 59). In a classroom-based learning environment, instructors might leave the social aspect of learning to the learners. Learners usually greet each other informally as they enter the classroom and strike up conversations as they wait for class to begin, or they meet after class. In an online environment, informal communications are more difficult to initiate because learners are missing the visual cues that indicate whether an individual is approachable. Social introductions therefore become the instructor's responsibility. If the instructor knows other experienced online learners in the environment, he or she may assign them a special role to play in the icebreaker, or even ask them to lead it. For example, an experienced online learner could serve as a greeter for students by sending a "good to meet you" response to others in the online class or could model responses for others in the learning environment.

CHARACTERISTICS OF AN EFFECTIVE ICEBREAKER

An icebreaker should not require anything more than the ability to express knowledge of self. It relates more to the personal life than the academic life of the learner. You might think of an icebreaker as representing the first few minutes you spend with a new acquaintance in a social setting. An icebreaker should humanize the technology-mediated learning experience so that trust can begin to be built among learners. This trust is vital in order for community interactions to occur in the future.

Secondary to the humanization process is the fact that an introductory, non-threatening interaction also breaks the ice of using technology to communicate for learners who are new to the online learning environment.

An icebreaker should be carefully planned, not left to chance. It sets the tone for future communications between learners; therefore, it should be fun, creative, and expressive. Table 5.1 lists elements to consider when evaluating the design of your icebreaker.

Table 5.1. Checklist for an Effective Icebreaker

	Yes/No	Comments
1. Is the activity fun and nonthreatening?		
2. Is it person-focused, not content-focused?		
3. Does it require learners to read one another's entries?		
4. Does it require the learner to find something in common with at least 10 percent of the learning community?		
5. Does it require a person to be imaginative or express genuine emotions or openness?		
6. Are learners required to respond to one another?		

Table 5.2. Icebreakers to Try

Activity	Asynchronous	Synchronous
Bingo	✓	
Classmate Quiz	✓	
Lineup	✓	✓
Lost in Space	✓	
Name That Movie	✓	
One Word	✓	✓
Portrait	✓	
Room with a View	✓	
Snowball	✓	✓
Things	✓	
Truths and Lies	✓	✓
What Kind of Animal?	✓	
Why Are We Together?	✓	✓

Bingo

Task:	Introductory exercise for the second week (or second session) of a course
Objective:	To introduce students and expedite creation of a community in a fun way
Author:	Jerry Linnins, Manager, Learning Operations, Bechtel Corporation, San Francisco, grlinnin@bechtel.com
Method:	Asynchronous

Instructions

You will be e-mailed an instructor-created bingo card with each class member's name in one square. We will play bingo based on last week's introductions, your previously submitted bio, and course content. Mark each square as you determine the correct name. You will have twenty-four hours to post your responses to a threaded discussion list. The instructor will post the correct responses at the end of the twenty-four-hour period. Winners, based on time submitted and number of correct responses, will be announced.

Activity Author's Note

It is amazing how much energy such a simple exercise creates. People talk about their discoveries for many hours, over many sessions. It really helps a group to bond.

The bingo game is fun and interactive and keeps the focus on learning—about the course material and about others in the class.

There are several inexpensive software programs that can be used to make bingo cards (for example, Zingo from Games by Thiagi), or you can just create a simple table in Microsoft Word. Both approaches work well.

Authors' Note

Another way to personalize this activity is to have the class member's digital photo with their name on the bingo card. This visual element helps students to have an increased sense of presence for themselves and their classmates.

Classmate Quiz

Task:	Introductory exercise for the beginning of a course
Objective:	To help students learn more about fellow classmates and their interests
Author:	Stuart E. Schwartz, Department of Special Education, University of Florida, ses@coe.ufl.edu
Method:	Asynchronous

Instructions

During the first week of class, you will be asked to post personal introductions to a threaded discussion area. You will be expected to read through each participant's posting before the next class session. A quiz will be held during the second week of class to see what you have learned about your fellow classmates. You will have three days to respond by e-mail to the instructor. Bonus points will be awarded for each correct response.

Activity Author's Note

I have all students post personal introductions during the first week of class, and I encourage everyone to read through them. To reinforce this activity, I hold a contest during the second week of class and ask questions such as "Who lives in Boston and works in a community center?" or "Who teaches special education classes in Tampa?" I ask questions that can be answered only by reading through all of the personal introductions. I give everyone three days to respond, then give bonus points to all who respond correctly. (Usually all answers are correct, of course.)

Authors' Note

A variation to this activity is to also have students include a digital photo or a clip art image of who they are at this point in their lives with an explanation. It is fun to revisit these objects at the end of the class to see if they have remained the same over the course of the class.

Lineup

Task:	Introductory exercise for the beginning of a course
Objective:	To allow students to get acquainted with their classmates' shared interests, backgrounds, and abilities in a nonthreatening atmosphere
Author:	J. Ana Donaldson, Ed.D., Walden University, ana.donaldson@waldenu.edu
Method:	Asynchronous or synchronous

Instructions

You will be asked to score yourself from 1 to 10 on the following items. A score of 1 indicates minimal knowledge or interest, and the top score of 10 signifies that you are very interested or ready to teach the subject. Enter your scores for each item on the discussion board or in the chat room as the question is presented.

1. I consider myself a sports expert.
2. Cooking is one of my hobbies.
3. I love to read.
4. I am interested in the subject matter of this course.
5. I feel comfortable with computers.

Once all scores have been entered, look for the individual with the score closest to yours. Introduce yourself to this individual, and see what other areas you may have in common. It is now your task to introduce this person to the group through a posting on the discussion board entitled "Introductions" by the end of the first week of the course. If no one introduces himself or herself to you by the middle of the first week, contact the instructor for assistance.

Activity Author's Note

It is fun to vary the list of questions for each class. Finding who has traveled the furthest from home in the last year, learned a new sport, or worn something unique for Halloween are all types of questions that encourage an active discussion.

Lost in Space

Task:	Introductory exercise for the beginning of a course
Objective:	To allow students to get acquainted with their classmates' shared interests, backgrounds, and abilities in a nonthreatening atmosphere
Author:	Rita-Marie Conrad, Ph.D., Florida State University, rita.conrad@fsu.edu
Method:	Synchronous

Instructions

Sometimes we learn more about people through their priorities than their standard introductions. Imagine you have been living on a space station for a period of one year. Suddenly the computers malfunction, and you have fifteen minutes to evacuate to a space shuttle before all life support systems fail. You will be allowed five items to take with you. As quickly as you can, type your name followed by the five items in the chat room. This is not the time for reflective thought. Just type as quickly as you can. Once all participants have entered their list, read through what has been entered. The facilitator will call each of you by name to explain why you chose your items.

Activity Author's Note

If the class is large, divide it randomly into teams and have each team conduct this exercise in its group chat room. Be sure to assign one person to facilitate the team and report the voting results when the large class reconvenes after this exercise.

Responses usually fall into the categories of personal, technology, and survival items.

Be prepared for a group who may state that they wouldn't take anything with them, their reasoning will be that if our society is technologically advanced enough to get us to the moon, then whatever we might need would be available in a digital back-up format. This has actually happened to Ana in one of her classes!

Name That Movie

Task: Introductory exercise for the beginning of a course
Objective: To describe a learner's life in an innovative way
Author: Doug Palm, Assistant Director of Resource Development, United Way of Dane County, dougp@uwdc.org; Bruce Jawer, Program Manager, IBM, jawer@us.ibm.com; Wendy MacColl, Director of Instructional Design, University of Arkansas Walton College of Business, wmaccoll@walton.uark.edu; Dan Reigel, Information Systems Consultant, Marshfield Clinic, reigel.dan@marshfield clinic.org; Melissa Kubly, Sr. Training Specialist, WPS Health Insurance, wps.mkubly@wpsic.com
Method: Asynchronous

Instructions

DAY 1: Post a 2–3 sentence response to the following:
If you were to write the score to the movie of your life, which two songs would you pick and why? Please pick one song that represents your life as a whole and another that gives a more recent picture.

DAY 2: Based on the answers to #1, suggest a movie title for each person followed by a one-sentence explanation of why you chose that title. Please include all titles in one posting.

DAY 3: Consider all the suggested titles for your movie. Select the one title that would best fit your movie followed by a 1–2 sentence explanation.

Author's Note

This activity needs to be carefully facilitated. With a diverse set of students, popular music and movies might not all be viewed in the same light. In one of our classes a student from Puerto Rico was associated with the movie *Evita*. The leader Eva Peron can be seen in either a positive or negative light. It was a relief when the student said she was honored to be associated with such a strong woman.

One Word

Task:	Introductory exercise for the beginning of a course
Objective:	To introduce a student's interests and self-perception to classmates in an innovative way
Authors:	Rita-Marie Conrad, Ph.D., Florida State University, rita.conrad@fsu.edu and J. Ana Donaldson, Ed.D., Walden University, ana.donaldson@waldenu.edu
Method:	Asynchronous or synchronous

Instructions

Asynchronously:

Think of one word that best describes you or your life. Enter your word and your name in the subject line of a discussion board entry, then explain why you chose that word in the body of the posting. Review the entries of others and find someone else whose word resonates with you. Reply to their message and try to find at least two additional nouns that the two of you have in common by the end of the week.

Synchronously:

Think of one word that describes you or your life. Post your word in the chat room as the facilitator "calls" your name. Once all names have been called, review the words and send a private message introducing yourself to an individual whose noun resonates with you. Try to come up with two more words that you have in common with that person.

Activity Author's Note

This is one activity that has expanded over the years. After the activity is completed, the words are posted under a digital picture of each student, and then a photo gallery of the class is posted to the class Web site. Ana has even gone a step further by using the individual words when assigning teams by creating a descriptive sentence describing the new collaborative group.

Portrait

Task:	Introductory exercise for the beginning of a course
Objective:	To introduce students' interests and self-perceptions to classmates in a fun and entertaining way
Author:	J. Ana Donaldson, Ed.D., Walden University, ana.donaldson@waldenu.edu
Method:	Asynchronous

Instructions

You are to create a self-portrait to share with your instructor and classmates. Artistic ability is not essential. Crayons and paper or a graphics program may be used. If you get desperate, you might use a picture in a magazine that best portrays who you are at this point in your life. A basic photograph of you will not be accepted. Once your picture is completed, transmit a digital image of your artistic endeavor as an attachment. Explain why you included the elements that you did and what influenced your decisions in creating your portrait.

Activity Author's Note

An effective reflective activity is an end-of-course montage of images representing what the student has learned with an explanation. Again, creativity and reflection are valued more than artistic ability for this task.

Room with a View

Task:	Introductory exercise for the beginning of a course
Objective:	To find commonalities with others in the learning community
Authors:	Joan Vandervelde, University of Northern Iowa, Director, Online Professional Development, vanderveldej@uni.edu; Chris Vadnais, Air Force Broadcasting Service, vadnais@host6.net; Simone Sandler, Senior Lecturer, Bar Ilan University, ssandler@mail.biu.ac.il; Charles Christison, University of Wisconsin-Platteville, Instructional Designer, chrischa@uwplatt.edu; Mike Levenhagen, Oshkosh Truck Corporation, Continuous Improvement Trainer, mlevenhagen@ oshtruck.com; Dennis O'Connor, Instructor, University of Northern Iowa, dennis.oconnor@uni.edu
Method:	Asynchronous

Instructions

Describe (in vivid detail) the view from your favorite window. Weave some autobiographical information into your "view." For example, "I'm looking out over our pool where my son learned to swim this weekend. It also overlooks a lake. When we lived in Arizona we dreamed about living by water and now that we are here in Florida that has become a reality." Read what others have written and respond to two peers' postings indicating why you would like to trade places for a day.

Author's Note

This is a great opportunity for students to receive extra credit for attaching a picture or graphic representation of their favorite place. Providing a link to a MapQuest location also gives students a clearer idea of where the room is located. If privacy is a concern, the view can describe where you would like to be if a genie magically answered all of your wishes.

Snowball

Task:	Introductory exercise for the beginning of a course
Objective:	To find commonalities with others in the learning community
Author:	Rita-Marie Conrad, Ph.D., Florida State University, rita.conrad@fsu.edu
Method:	Asynchronous or synchronous

Instructions

Have one person enter a basic introduction of himself or herself, including his or her interests. A second person must then enter an introduction of himself or herself and find one thing in common with the first person. A third person then enters his or her introduction and finds one thing in common with the first person and the second person. Each of the rest of the class members then enters an introduction and must find something in common with at least three other people in the class. The first person, in turn, must respond to at least three people with whom he or she has something in common. The second person must respond to at least two additional people. The third person must respond to at least one additional person.

Author's Activity Note

Be aware that using this activity with a large group will turn a "Snowball" into an "Avalanche"! Consider using this activity in groups no larger than ten. You could break the class into "getting to know you" groups randomly or use this activity after teams have been assigned. This task can also be very effective when the introductions are done through the creation of simple YouTube or video casts.

Things

Task:	Introductory exercise for the beginning of a course
Objective:	To introduce students' interests and background to classmates in an innovative way
Author:	J. Ana Donaldson, Ed.D., Walden University, ana.donaldson@waldenu.edu
Method:	Asynchronous

Instructions

Find an object or a digital image that represents who you are or why you are taking this course or even what your research interests might be. Post a description of the object on the discussion board and explain why you chose that particular object. Attach a digital image of your object: a scanned image, digital picture, or Web-linked image, for example. Include a brief description of your expectations for the class in the explanation of your object.

Author's Activity Note

Extra credit is possible for a student willing to create a course montage of the objects chosen. This group image can then be placed on the course Web site.

Truths and Lies

Task: Introductory exercise for the beginning of a course

Objective: To introduce a student's interests and background to classmates in a fun and challenging way

Author: Darek Jarmola, Ph.D., Oklahoma Wesleyan University, djarmola@okwu.edu

Method: Asynchronous or synchronous

Instructions

Enter two truthful statements and one falsehood about yourself onto the discussion board (or into the chat room). Each member of the group should then try to distinguish the truths from the lie. What makes this activity fun is to be as outrageous as possible while sharing a bit of who you really are with your fellow participants. Once all responses have been received, post your truths and explain why you chose them to share.

Author's Note

This task can be expanded to require that students document their "outrageous" truths. Encourage the group to have fun with this activity. As the instructor, you might want to model your own Truths and Lies. Just make sure that nothing is posted by the group that they wouldn't want to share with their grandmothers.

What Kind of Animal?

Task: Introductory exercise for the beginning of a course

Objective: To provide an informal way for participants to learn about each other and begin working together

Author: Dave Searcey, Instructional Designer, Air Education and Training Command, USAF, dave.searcey@randolph.af.mil

Method: Asynchronous

Instructions

1. Choose an animal that best represents you. Put your name and the name of the animal in the subject line of the discussion post and list four characteristics of the animal you have chosen.
2. Find someone else who chose an animal that shares two of the characteristics of your animal. Contact them and together create a new animal that has your two shared characteristics and two new characteristics. Name the animal.
3. Post the name of your new animal, as well as both of your names in the subject line of the discussion entry and then list the four characteristics of this animal.
4. Provide feedback to several of your peers on the animals they have created.

Author's Note

This activity has resulted in some amazing animal combinations. One example is the Zebaffpuss. That poor fellow had the stripes of a zebra, the neck of a giraffe, and the duckbill of a platypus. A variation on this might be to discuss choices for vegetables and then find a recipe to combine the selections.

Why Are We Together?

Task: Introductory exercise for the beginning of a course

Objective: To provide an informal way for participants to learn about one another's interests and reasons for enrolling in the course

Author: Rita-Marie Conrad, Ph.D., Florida State University, rita.conrad@fsu.edu

Method: Asynchronous or synchronous

Instructions

Prior to this activity, you completed an initial profile form for the instructor. Based on your initial profile, you will be assigned to a discussion group of four to five people. Using the discussion board, group area, or assigned chat room, your group must discover why its members were put together. Also, are there any other things that group members have in common that were not included in the profile survey? You will be asked to share your common reason with the other groups.

Author's Note

When Ana has used this activity it has caused more discussion than any others in this section. Her choice is to create a group that includes someone identified as having leadership qualities, someone comfortable with technology, and the rest added based on a toss of a coin. It is amazing how hard the students look for nonexistent connections. The outcome of this task is the vast amount of information that they share.

Peer Partnership and Team Activities

Once learners have gotten to know one another on a social level through Phase 1 introductory activities, academic peer interactions can begin. The overall purpose of pairing learners for an activity is to help them develop and exchange academic ideas with an unseen peer.

Peer exchanges also require that learners critique one another tactfully and helpfully. Working with only one online peer initially helps a learner develop critiquing skill before working in a group. This skill needs to be practiced more in an online environment than in a classroom-based environment because visual and aural cues are missing, so text-based criticisms, even when they are constructive, can be construed as overly harsh.

Peer partnership activities also provide an additional opportunity for learners new to the online environment to become more comfortable with the technology before they have to use it for larger group communication.

Dyads (two students working together) can be formed either by the instructor or by the learners themselves, based on the introductory activity. A peer partnership activity should be simple. It could be an individual assignment that is then shared with a peer, or it could require discussion with a peer and a collaborative response that is posted to the entire learning community.

Depending on the assignment, critiquing guidelines can range from very simple to extremely complex and detailed. An example of a simple critiquing guideline is as follows: "List three things you liked about your peer's assignment and three things that need improvement." More complex guidelines might be something like the following: "Consider each of the statements made by your peer and provide feedback concerning the number of issues raised and the quality of the argument." Critiquing guidelines should be set by the instructor and should be based on the expected instructional outcomes of the activity.

Table 6.1 provides some guidelines for creating peer activities.

MOVING DYADS TO TEAMS

After a peer partnership activity has been completed, the dyads can be combined into larger teams for cooperative activities. Using dyads first allows an instructor to see how well peers work together and, in some cases, how learners view collaboration. If peer partners have not worked well together, the instructor may choose to assign the peers to separate groups. This has the potential to minimize problems that could affect the work of an entire team.

Boettcher and Conrad (2010) identify the following aspects to consider when assigning teams:

Table 6.1. Checklist for an Effective Peer Partnership Activity

	Yes/No	Comments
1. Is the activity academically oriented?		
2. Is it content-focused?		
3. Does it require learners to read one another's entries?		
4. Does it require that peers express what they agreed with or liked about each other's work?		
5. Does it require that peers express what they would improve in each other's work?		

- Amount of content familiarity or expertise of students
- Types of professional contexts in which the students are working
- Types and number of roles the group needs
- Learner goals for the course experience
- Culture, gender, and age (it is often beneficial to mix these)
- Students' online work habits
- Time zones where students are located (p. 128)

It is vital that a team activity require an interweaving of thoughts and not simply be a result of individual thoughts and actions. Team projects should require all members to be active in the development and decision-making process and to be individually accountable for their contributions. This can be accomplished through the team member evaluations discussed in Chapter Three. See Table 6.2 for more suggestions on creating team activities.

Table 6.2. Checklist for an Effective Team Activity

	Yes/No	Comments
1. Does the activity consist of more than just questions and answers?		
2. Is it content-focused?		
3. Does it require learners to respond to each other and build on one another's thoughts?		
4. Does it require team members to demonstrate critical thinking?		
5. Is the team required to produce a synthesized response or end product?		
6. Are team members held individually accountable for their contributions to the discussion or project?		

Table 6.3. Peer Partnership and Team Activities to Try

Activity	Asynchronous	Synchronous
Contest of the Week	✓	✓
Dyad Debate	✓	
Group Contract	✓	✓
How's My Driving?	✓	✓
Medieval Shield	✓	✓
Progressive Project	✓	
Structured Chat		✓
Structured Discussion	✓	

Contest of the Week

Task: Peer activity that contributes additional information on the week's topic

Objective: To work with a partner to acquire new information on the class's current topic

Author: Stuart E. Schwartz, Department of Special Education, University of Florida, ses@coe.ufl.edu

Method: Asynchronous or synchronous

Instructions

Contest #1: With your peer partner, find a Web site for a national organization that relates to our topic. Post the URL and a very brief description of the organization.

Contest #2: With your peer partner, determine the name of a well-known person, such as a politician or movie star, who has some relationship to the week's topic. Explain how the person relates to the topic.

Activity Author's Note

I use this activity to encourage participation and to get new ideas flowing. I have a contest each week. Each contest is different and has a clearly established deadline. In each case, I don't allow duplicates, so the students have to read all of the other submissions. Contest winners get bonus points.

Dyad Debate

Task:	To discuss a controversial issue with a peer online
Objective:	To introduce students to the idea of exchanging oppositional thoughts online
Authors:	Mona P. Ternus, RN, C, Ph.D., Old Dominion University, mternus@ mickey.aum.edu and Debbie R. Faulk, RN, Ph.D., Auburn University Montgomery School of Nursing, dfaulk@mickey.aum.edu
Method:	Asynchronous

Instructions

Using the threaded discussion area, debate two of the following issues with your assigned discussion partner: (1) Should illegal immigrants be included in health care policy regulations and benefits? (2) Should Medicaid pay for elective abortions? (3) Should the federal government decide whether physician-assisted suicide is legal? (4) Should fetal tissue be used for research? (5) Is health care a right that should be accessible and available to everyone regardless of their ability to pay?

   Each of you should post a summary of one of your debates under the discussion area for issue 1, issue 2, issue 3, and so on. Read the summaries others have written and comment on at least two of the other teams' debates.

Author's Note

Debate questions can be tailored to your field of study. A great source for finding opinions is to reference a blog posting of a leader in the field. You might even have the pair post their final thoughts to that blog and have the key person in the field become part of the discussion.

Group Contract

Task: Team building exercise

Objective: To determine the code of conduct for a team

Author: Mary Dereshiwsky, Northern Arizona University, statcatmd@earthlink.net

Method: Asynchronous or Synchronous

Instructions

Now that you've been assigned to a group, it's time to determine how your group will operate. Our syllabus contains a discussion of some things you might want to negotiate with your teammates. A good group code of conduct and contract will include, but are not necessarily limited to, the following items:

1. How will you communicate? Will you post notes and updates for one another in your group discussion areas? Will you communicate via a mass e-mail list, where anything that one group member sends is received by all? Will you meet in person? Any or all of the preceding?

2. How often will you be expected to check for updates from your group members?

3. Will there be a permanent group leader, or will this task be rotated in some way?

4. Who will be assigned to post the group's assignment solution in your discussion area per the due date policy in our syllabus? Will one person be the poster or recorder, or will group members take turns posting assignment solutions?

5. What will be your group's policy, if any, on absences and covering for one another if need be?

6. *Important:* What policy will you have in place to resolve any intragroup conflict that may arise (for example, if a group member neglects to carry out his or her delegated duties to post the assignment on time, or if a group member is not receiving or responding to group updates as often as expected in item 2 above)? You may use me (the instructor) as a higher court of appeals—I will always be happy to moderate and intervene if need be—but you will first be expected to document for me that you implemented your initial conflict resolution plans per your contract and to update me on the outcomes of your own attempts to resolve the conflict.

Continued

You will want to begin communicating with your group members as soon as possible to work out the final draft of the group code of conduct or contract, so that the designated group member can post it in your group's work area by the due date.

Author's Note

This is a critical first task for the newly formed group in Phase III. If you plan on keeping a dyad in Phase II beyond a week, then you may also consider a contract for their interactions. If problems occur, it is important to keep reminding the groups of their contracts as the course progresses. That contract allows most groups to resolve their conflicts before the instructor is called in to intervene.

How's My Driving?

Task: Formative course evaluation

Objective: To provide team feedback to an instructor

Author: Marjorie Henderson, University of Illinois, mjwh@uiuc.edu or
                  m.henderson@insightbb.com

Method: Asynchronous or Synchronous

Instructions

As your instructor, it is important to me that you learn the material in this course, but it is of equal importance that I present the material and guide your learning process in the most meaningful way possible, creating a learning environment that will help you to achieve the desired outcomes. If you promise to be professional and candid about my teaching, I promise to use your feedback to strengthen my teaching and possibly change the course significantly based on your suggestions. In a student-centered teaching and learning environment, the instructor often learns from the students. At the beginning of this course, I asked you to evaluate the design and structure of the course Web site. Now I would like to know how you feel about how I am facilitating the course and about how you are learning.

Task: In groups of four or five, your task is to collaborate and create a summary that provides specific feedback on what you like or do not like about this course, including what you feel needs improvement and your ideas on how to carry out the improvement. Although some of you obviously talk to each other and express your attitudes about the course from time to time, this method of evaluation has the unique advantage of letting each of you know what your peers think about the course's strengths and weaknesses.

Process: You are to spend the next week discussing and formulating your thoughts. Appoint someone from your group to post a 300-to-400-word summary to the appropriate discussion forum. During the following week, I would like each of you to respond to at least two other groups' summaries.

Resources: The resources for this project include you, your class colleagues, other courses you have taken or are aware of, (for comparison or as examples), this course, and me!

Evaluation: Each team member will get ten activity points for completing this project; any other method of grading might influence you to compliment my teaching rather than provide a substantive evaluation tool that can actually help my teaching. Once I have had a chance to look over your summaries and

Continued

discussion postings, I will formulate a response to provide you with my reaction to your suggestions and my plans for implementing those suggestions to improve the course. Since this is a professional communication course, my response may include general comments and suggestions (not addressing any particular team) regarding appropriate tone and professionalism in a project of this type, which, you may recall from Unit 1, is especially important when our correspondence may include some negative elements. I respect your opinions as professional students, and I look forward to your feedback.

Author's Note

It is critical that the instructor respond to the students' comments within 24–48 hours and that suggested modifications are addressed as soon as possible. If the suggestions are not possible, be sure to explain why.

Medieval Shield

Task:	Team building exercise
Objective:	To help team members determine the expertise they bring to a team
Author:	J. Ana Donaldson, Ed.D., Walden University, ana.donaldson@waldenu.edu
Method:	Asynchronous and Synchronous

Instructions

Find various graphics that represent the skills you bring to a team. Share and discuss them with your team either in your group's chat room or discussion thread.

As a team, build a graphic representation of a medieval shield with all the symbols of expertise on your team. Post it in the discussion group or add it to your team's profile page.

Author's Note

It is a good idea to also post the group graphic to the home page so all can share. This can lead to the group creating their own team name incorporating the ideas from the shield. You could even go a step further with the medieval theme and ask learners to designate their positions in the "kingdom" as an aid for assigning group roles. Roles might include: Ruler (King/Queen), Court Jester, Knight of the Round Table, Scribe, or any others that might apply.

Progressive Project

Task: Peer partner critique

Objective: To enable students to critique peers

Author: Gretchen Bartelson, Northwest Iowa Community College,
GBart@nwicc.edu

Method: Asynchronous

Instructions

Choose a topic for debate from the list provided. Write three pro arguments and the supporting points for those arguments. E-mail your work to your peer partner, who should write three con arguments and the supporting points for those arguments. Submit the work to the instructor, who will send it to another peer pair to evaluate. E-mail the project and the evaluation from the other team to the instructor, who will evaluate the entire project.

Activity Author's Note

I like this exercise for several reasons. First, it works well in an asynchronous environment. Second, people can be evaluated for the work that they do, and I don't have to try to sift out who did or didn't do the work. Finally, the evaluation component is very important because it is a good exercise in critical thinking. Students are usually much harder on themselves than I am.

Structured Chat

Task: Chat-room discussion of a paper from current literature on the class topic

Objective: To discuss salient points from the literature

Author: Evelyn Farrior, Ph.D., Eastern Carolina University, farriore@mail.ecu.edu

Method: Synchronous

Instructions

Read the assigned paper before chat time. Respond when a question is addressed to you. ("I don't know" is permitted.) Other students may add to the response after the person addressed has answered. Questions directed to the instructor are allowed.

Activity Author's Note

Students are scheduled to chat in groups of ten or less in one-hour time slots. Chat is required, and each student receives a participation grade. Every student is given a chance to give their input, even the slow typists. I, as the instructor, prepare by typing my questions and the expected answers into a document that is open on my computer. I copy the questions and expected answers, if needed, from the word-processed document and paste them into the chat room. This copying and pasting allows me to quickly move through chat sessions on the same topic. The questions are the same for each chat group.

I have been amazed at the feel I get for the level of understanding in the class. After initial nervousness about trying to answer questions by typing, the students say the chats are informative and fun. This method seems to work well with both graduates and undergraduates.

Structured Discussion

Task: Participation in three of nine discussion groups

Objective: Make substantive comments on a chosen topic

Authors: Mona P. Ternus, RN, C, Ph.D., Old Dominion University, mternus@ mickey.aum.edu and Debbie R. Faulk, RN, Ph.D., Auburn University Montgomery School of Nursing, dfaulk@mickey.aum.edu

Method: Asynchronous

Instructions

You are required to participate in three of nine discussion groups. Consider the readings, and offer a substantive comment that supports at least one point presented and a comment that refutes at least one point presented. Support your comments with solid reasoning. This means that you need to include a rationale for the idea you are supporting; as well as a rationale for your stance against the point that you are refuting. In addition, you need to comment on at least one other student's point of view.

If you are the first student to post in the discussion area, enter your viewpoint on the question, then return later to comment on another student's viewpoint (agree or disagree), including a rationale for your comment.

You can post one long comment, or you can post your points separately in three postings (support an idea, refute an idea, and comment on a student's point of view). You must post your comments within the week assigned to the discussion of that topic.

Grading Criteria for Discussion Postings

- Substantive comment, with rationale, that supports at least one point presented in the readings: 40 points

- Substantive comment, with rationale, that refutes at least one point presented in the readings: 40 points

- Substantive comment, with rationale, that supports or refutes a student's point of view: 20 points

Author's Note

This is a great activity to do on a blog. Post the original discussion topic with supporting information and then request comments from class members. Links to relevant blogs also add new perspectives to the discussion topic. Including a RSS feed capability also lets you know when additional comments have been added to the blog.

Reflective Activities

O ne of the major components of an engaged learning educational approach is reflection. Reflection is "where we can find the connections between our operational assumptions and our behaviors, decisions, and plans; where we can construct our identities and integrate different frameworks of practice" (Mentkowski & Associates, 2000, p. 265). It is "the central dynamic in intentional learning, problem solving, and validity testing through rational discourse" (Mezirow, 1991, p. 99).

Reflection can provide insight for instructors on their teaching and for students on their learning. Reflective feedback allows instructors to evaluate the effectiveness of the students' experiences in the course. This information can be used to continually modify the course to better meet not only the stated learning objectives but also the needs of learners. In addition, reflection allows students to gain insight into their individual activity outcomes and apply that knowledge to their learning experience.

Reflective activities can be conducted individually or in a group. Asking students to maintain a document, such as a reflective journal, in which their thoughts are recorded throughout a course, is an effective way to track individual experiences. Instructors may wish to read the journals on a weekly basis, but they should wait until at least the third week (in a twelve-to-sixteen-week course) to ask for journal submissions. Prior to the third week, most journal entries are filled with the frustrations of dealing with unfamiliar technology and expectations. Waiting until the last week of class to ask for a journal submission may result in a document that is patched together the night before the due date. Monthly submissions work best in most situations.

A final reflective activity conducted in a group not only provides closure but allows participants to share their perceptions and thoughts on the collective experience. The instructor may take a humorous approach with the "Bumper Sticker" activity from this section or choose a more serious tone with the "Summary Words" activity.

CHARACTERISTICS OF AN EFFECTIVE REFLECTIVE ACTIVITY

An effective reflective activity requires students to share a synthesis of the learning experience. Participants should be encouraged to share genuine emotions in a nonthreatening environment. A sense of fun and encouragement of imagination are components of many effective reflective activities. Other reflective activities may require students to describe how a situation had personal value for them. It is also beneficial if learners can provide feedback that will be useful to the instructor in future course development and instructional opportunities.

Making meaning out of a learning situation requires adequate time to contemplate the experience and synthesize it within the context of other newly acquired knowledge. The instructor must encourage this contemplation to take place as part of the course, and the learners must find time in their own busy lives to conduct this reflection. Activities that are done quickly are reactive, not reflective. In most cases, asynchronous activities accommodate deeper reflection than synchronous activities. However, synchronous sessions can be used to share reflections that have been prepared beforehand.

Use the checklist in Table 7.1 when developing your own reflective activities.

Table 7.1. Checklist for an Effective Reflective Activity

	Yes/No	Comments
1. Does the activity ask for a synthesis of the learning experience?		
2. Does it require the learner to share his or her experiences?		
3. Does it require the learner to provide helpful feedback that will be useful to the instructor in future course development?		
4. Does it allow for honest and open responses?		
5. Does it require a person to be imaginative or to express genuine emotions or openness?		
6. Is the activity insightful and nonthreatening?		
7. Will the activity be completed over several days or weeks in the course?		

Table 7.2. Reflective Activities to Try

Activity	Asynchronous	Synchronous
Aha!	✓	
Bumper Sticker	✓	
Critical Insight	✓	
I Didn't Know That	✓	
IRAs	✓	
More Words to Lead By	✓	
Picture	✓	
Summary Words	✓	✓

Aha!

Task:	Reflective exercise to be done on an ongoing basis during a course or unit
Objective:	To provide an innovative way for students to share their thoughts and experiences
Author:	Rita-Marie Conrad, Ph.D., Florida State University, rita.conrad@fsu.edu
Method:	Asynchronous

Instructions

During your time in this course you may experience what is termed an "Aha" moment—a moment when something you have been reading or contemplating makes sense with an unexpected clarity. You are asked to keep a journal of these moments while a member of the class. Periodically during the course, you will be asked to share your "Aha's" with the other class participants. A compilation of all such moments will be due at the end of the course.

Activity Author's Note

Making meaning of course content is sometimes a series of mini-epiphanies. Asking students to document these moments and share them with the class can encourage discussion and enrich the learning community that has been established. Too often students tend to see this task as a course journal or just an extended form of class notes. Ask them not to list what happened during the class but rather to share the insights and transformative experiences that were triggered by the class readings or related to class discussions.

Bumper Sticker

Task:	Reflective exercise for the end of a course or unit
Objective:	To provide an innovative way for students to share their thoughts and experiences in the course
Author:	Sharon Smaldino, Northern Illinois University, ssmaldino@niu.edu
Method:	Asynchronous

Instructions

You are asked to reflect on your experience as a member of this class. If you had to sum up your thoughts on the experience or the knowledge you have gained, how would they be stated on a bumper sticker? You will have one week to e-mail your response to the instructor. Extra points will be awarded if you actually create a graphic representation of the bumper sticker and e-mail it as an attachment.

Activity Author's Note

This activity was adapted from *101 Ways to Make Training Active* by Mel Silberman and Karen Lawson (1995).

Everyone that has used this activity has enjoyed the task. It has provided many insights and a lot of fun.

Author's Note

The parameter is that students have less than ten words to describe the experience. Prizes can be offered to those who make the biggest statement with the fewest words. You could create a bumper sticker gallery of all entries with a link from the homepage. An additional idea is to ask students to describe the type of car on which you would find the bumper sticker and why that car was chosen.

Critical Insight

Task: Reflective exercise for the middle of a course or unit

Objective: To get students to read actively in the textbook and provide an opportunity for them to explore an area of interest in more depth

Author: Susan Davis Allen, MS, RD, Facilitator, Center for Learning Innovation, Southwest Wisconsin Technical College, sallen@southwest.tec.wi.us

Method: Asynchronous

Instructions

1. Choose one chapter of the textbook that interests you.
2. Choose one article from a newspaper, journal, or other periodical that represents the concepts of that chapter (or a portion of the chapter).
3. Choose three Web sites (give the URLs) that provide useful information about the concepts of that chapter (or a portion of the chapter).
4. Write three to five paragraphs that describe why you chose that chapter and the article and the Web sites to represent that chapter.
5. Write one question that came to your mind as you were completing this assignment.
6. Post your assignment summary and your question to the discussion board.
7. The written material must meet the criteria specified for grammar and spelling and critical thinking.

Activity Author's Note

I have been teaching online for almost three years. During that time, I have improved my guidance of discussions, but I wanted an activity that also got the learners involved with the course textbook. I designed this activity, and it worked well both to get learners involved with their textbook and to provide a discussion platform. This activity is used in the course Professional Development for Dietary Managers, and the textbook is *Proof of Performance* by Rich Nelles.

Author's Note

An additional item to expand this task is to have the student provide at least one example that demonstrates the concept of the chapter along with an explanation that supports the choice.

I Didn't Know That

Task:	Reflective exercise at middle of course or a specific unit
Objective:	To give students an opportunity to think about what they are learning and contribute to the class discussion
Author:	Stuart E. Schwartz, Department of Special Education, University of Florida, ses@coe.ufl.edu
Method:	Asynchronous

Instructions

Using the "I Didn't Know That" discussion thread, post something new that you've learned this week, either from another student, from the text, or from class discussions. Indicate how you will use the new information or skill.

Activity Author's Note

This posting counts toward their minimum number of discussion contributions, and it allows them to indicate what they've learned and how they will use the new information or skill.

Author's Note:

An addition might be "I Can Use This." Explain how this new information will make a difference in how students perform a task or perceive a concept. The goal is not only to recognize that learning is taking place but how it can have a transformative effect on the student.

IRAs (Insights, Resource Sharing, and Applications)

Task: Reflective exercise for the beginning of a course module
Objective: To encourage students to learn actively and to share their insights and knowledge
Author: Dave Johnson, DNS, RN, CS, Professor of Nursing, University of Saint Francis—Fort Wayne, IN, DJohnson@sf.edu
Method: Asynchronous

Instructions

Before starting the case scenario discussion for each module, you will post an IRA (Insights, Resource, and Application) in the discussion board, as follows:

3 INSIGHTS (I). Create bullet points from the readings (approximately one sentence each). This is your insight; grab hold of it and share it. Insights are like the tail end of dreams; they fade. Grab them during your readings and be prepared to summarize them briefly on the discussion board.

1 RESOURCE (R). In addition to the assigned reading, share one other resource that amplifies themes from the assigned reading. Note a book, article, news item, Web site, or contemporary film with similar themes, ideas, or thoughts. These can be resources that you have used in the past or that you have found this semester. Cite your resource using APA format, and give no more than one or two sentences about how this resource is relevant to the assigned readings or discussion.

1 APPLICATION (A). Provide an example from current clinical or past experience (approximately one paragraph). This captures your thoughts about how the reading is related to something that is currently happening or something from your clinical past. Does the reading validate your insights about a particular event or situation or help to clarify what a different approach may have looked like?

Activity Author's Note

I teach an online nursing leadership and management course for registered nurses going back to school for their B.S.N. This semester I developed the "IRA approach" to help engage students by having them make learning "investments" before they enter the discussion board. My course is developed around seven modules, and students complete an IRA at the beginning of each module.

Students are to have assigned readings completed on the date of the scheduled topic and are expected to take the role of self-directed learner. Additional outside readings are encouraged. The ability to critically think, evaluate, and share perceptions is an expectation for all students.

More Words to Lead By

Task:	Reflective activity to be used throughout a course
Objective:	To provide an opportunity for students to take a break from the rigors of the course
Author:	Mary I. Dereshiwsky, Ph.D., Associate Professor, Educational Leadership and Research, Center for Excellence in Education, Northern Arizona University, statcatmd@earthlink.net
Method:	Asynchronous

Instructions

You are encouraged to read the contents of the folder titled "More Words to Lead By." Items are posted twice weekly to this folder and contain positive stories, poems, or quotes centered on a common theme. This material is provided for you to read, reflect on, and enjoy.

Activity Author's Note

I create a read-only folder in my asynchronous classroom area called "More Words to Lead By." This title ties in with my academic department, Educational Leadership and Research. I also create a catchy title for the cluster that reflects its theme; for example, I have a trio of time-management pieces that I call "It's About Time." I usually post this cluster toward the end of the semester when students might be feeling a bit harried and hurried. I find that one-half to two-thirds of my graduate research students read these "More Words to Lead By" posts. I also usually get fan mail from students telling me how much they enjoy these pieces; it's a nice visual break from the tough stuff of research concepts that they are learning online with me. I also believe this helps humanize me to my students.

Author's Note

In the frantic pace of most online courses, it is good to occasionally take some time to breathe. Every few weeks, consider posting a humorous YouTube video or a link to a favorite song or image for students to enjoy.

Picture

Task:	Reflective exercise for the end of course or a specific unit
Objective:	To provide feedback from students to the instructor and other classmates on their class experience
Author:	J. Ana Donaldson, Ed.D., Walden University, ana.donaldson@waldenu.edu
Method:	Asynchronous

Instructions

You are to complete this assignment as a member of a group. Your group is to find or create a picture that is related to the course content. Send an e-mail message of 100 to 200 words to the instructor, stating why your perception of the content of this picture has been altered because of what you have learned during the course. Attach a digital image of the picture to your report.

Activity Author's Note

You may want to preselect the images that your groups analyze. Pictures that tell a story, elicit strong emotions, or directly relate to the course content are recommended. Comparisons between group reactions to a common image could be an additional step in this activity.

Summary Words

Task:	Reflective exercise at end of course or a specific unit
Objective:	To provide feedback to the instructor and other classmates on the shared experience
Author:	J. Ana Donaldson, Ed.D., Walden University, ana.donaldson@waldenu.edu
Method:	Synchronous entry, asynchronous reflection

Instructions

Take a few minutes to reflect on your reactions to our completed class (or identified unit). What word or expression comes to mind? Enter each word or expression into the subject line of a discussion thread. Send as many words as you can think of in five minutes. This is not the time to analyze your input; just key and send.
Wait twenty-four hours, then review the responses of your classmates. Choose one word or expression that speaks directly to you. Post a response to the discussion that explains why this word has special meaning in defining the class experience for you.

Activity Author's Note

This activity has been modified from one created for the American Red Cross HIV/AIDS training materials. This can also be done in a face-to-face final class or professional development setting. The modifications are that everyone is given 15–20 scraps of paper, one for each word. When students are done with writing each word on their scraps, place all words in an area where everyone can view all contributions. Participants are then asked to choose one word that "speaks" to them. They then take terms sharing the word chosen and why. The fun part of this is that most students chose a different word from their own.

Authentic Activities

One of the important tenets of engaged learning is that learning activities should have meaning beyond the learning environment. "The process of connecting the learning gained from everyday life to the learning of the course not only creates a deeper sense of meaning for the participants but it validates them as people who possess knowledge and who can apply what they know in other contexts" (Palloff & Pratt, 1999, p. 116). This is especially important in an online environment, where our learning objectives and the characteristics of our students have been changing. We are discovering that many of our online learners are what we once called nontraditional students. They often bring a wealth of life experiences to the course that can be used as a springboard for meaningful activities.

One role of instructors is to provide students with meaningful experiences that will have relevance in their lives beyond the instructional situation. Asking a surgeon to practice an operation on a cadaver is far more beneficial than having him or her practice the same techniques on a watermelon or a frog. In the same way, an instructor can provide a situation that mimics reality but provides a safe environment in which both success and failure are possible.

CHARACTERISTICS OF AN EFFECTIVE AUTHENTIC ACTIVITY

The primary characteristic of an authentic activity is that it simulates an actual situation. Another important aspect is that it draws on the previous experiences of the learners. Students' problem-solving power increases enormously when they are asked to work collaboratively in an area where they share interests and experiences. In this situation, the task itself can become the motivating force.

It is helpful to remember that some of the best lessons are learned from failure and subsequent reflection. When there is acceptance of learning from mistakes, students will take meaningful and creative chances. Just as someone learning to ride a bicycle may need to fall a few times prior to mastery, it is important to allow a student to fail within any learning situation. Challenges should always be present and success should be achieved through repeated experiences.

To be effective, the activity must have value outside the learning setting and should build skills that can be used beyond the life of the course. The ultimate goal is to build lifelong learners who can take advantage of opportunities to apply knowledge and skills gained in their courses and identify new knowledge that they need to develop in the future. Whenever possible, the authentic activity should also have a means of being implemented and evaluated. For example, planning a community project has value beyond the course when suggestions can actually be implemented—such as by submitting a grant proposal. This is a demonstrable expression of success beyond the classroom.

Table 8.1 provides some guidelines for planning authentic activities.

Table 8.1. Checklist for an Effective Authentic Activity

	Yes/No	Comments
1. Is the activity authentic?		
2. Does it require learners to work collaboratively and use their experiences as a starting point?		
3. Are learners allowed to learn from their mistakes?		
4. Does the activity have value beyond the learning setting?		
5. Does the activity build skills that can be used beyond the life of the course?		
6. Do learners have a way to implement their outcomes in a meaningful way?		

Table 8.2. Authentic Activities to Try

Activity	Asynchronous	Synchronous
Case Study	✓	
Celebrity Chat	✓	
Cross-Region Discussion	✓	
Team Problem Solving	✓	
Pyramid	✓	
Social Responsibility	✓	

Case Study

Task:	Authentic task for learning content by means of case studies
Objective:	To help students incorporate evidence-based practice guidelines into real-life situations
Author:	C. Lynne Ostrow, Ed.D., RN, Chair, Department of Health Restoration, West Virginia University School of Nursing, Morgantown, WV, lostrow@hsc.wvu.edu
Method:	Asynchronous

Instructions

The class will be assigned seven case studies. Each student will work up one case study within an assigned group of three students. The instructor will provide the case studies, along with specific questions to be researched, at the beginning of the semester. The group responsible for a specific case study must post the case study and complete answers to the research questions one week in advance of the scheduled online chat on that case study. The rest of the students in the class are encouraged to respond to the case study with their own thoughtful responses: what they have seen clinically, new research, local practice guidelines, or questions that they still have about the topic. Members of the presenting group will respond to their classmates throughout the week. The instructor will read the bulletin board every day and comment on the dialogue as appropriate. Students can earn bonus points for their thoughtful responses.

Activity Author's Note

This activity worked very well this year. I was impressed with the quality of the research that case study groups did and how many varied and interesting additions were made to the case studies throughout the weeklong discussions. Students rated this part of the class the highest and felt that they now knew experts in their state in the seven content areas that the case studies covered—asthma, hypertension, and so on.

I have learned that it is important to tie up the weekly loose ends. At completion of the weekly posting, all discussion is pulled together; any areas that are still fuzzy to some students are clarified, and so on.

Celebrity Chat

Task:	Authentic task for a group or class to chat with an expert in the field of study
Objective:	To provide an alternative way for students to understand course content from an expert
Author:	J. Ana Donaldson, Ed.D., Walden University, ana.donaldson@waldenu.edu
Method:	Synchronous

Instructions

1. An individual who is a recognized expert in our course focus or current topic's content has agreed to be a celebrity guest in two weeks. Your assigned group will work together to develop three questions for our guest expert. One week prior to the scheduled celebrity chat, e-mail your three questions to me, the chat session's facilitator, for review and approval.

2. On the evening of the chat, you will be expected to log into the class chat room at a specified time. Plan on the first fifteen minutes to be devoted to group chat and preparation for the arrival of our celebrity guest.

3. Our guest has agreed to be online with us for one hour. We will need to use that time wisely. Each group in turn will post their questions and the class will respond with discussion. It is important that you pay close attention to the discourse since your questions may already be answered within a previous response. After one hour, our expert will leave the chat area but you are expected to continue online for an additional thirty minutes. As facilitator, I will lead a discussion on your reaction to the information that has been shared. Focus will be on how the dialog supported our previous course instruction. Also, be prepared to share what responses from our guest might have surprised you.

Activity Author's Note

The key to this activity is finding the appropriate guest expert. You might want to consider the course's textbook author, a recognized name in the field, or an instructor teaching the same subject matter at a different location. The required submission of group questions and pre- and post-class times ensure that the guest's time is focused on content and the class is focused on preparation and reflection. Advance notice also allows the guest to have responses developed to allow for a simple "cut and paste."

Cross-Region Discussion

Task: Authentic activity to allow students from different locations to interact and to reflect on the experience

Objective: To emphasize the importance of culture and cultural diversity

Author: Donna Darden, Tennessee Technological University, DKDarden@charter.net

Method: Asynchronous

Instructions

A question has been posted to our class discussion board. Both our class and another class from a different location will share in this discussion. You will have a period of one week to respond to the stated question. At the end of the week, e-mail a message to your instructor about the differences and similarities you observed in the responses of the two groups. Include a suggested question for the next week's discussion board activity.

Activity Author's Note

Here's something that has not worked yet, but I think it will, if I can find the right person to work with. The idea is good; I just need another group that's into electronic discussion.

I teach introductory sociology. One of the most basic ideas we have to get across is the importance of culture in our lives, and the concept that culture varies even within our own country. I'm on my second try at setting up a joint discussion board with students from another region of the country. I tried with the prompt "What I did last Saturday," and my students, who got hooked early on discussion boards, posted away, but I've not yet found a group to join us. Today, a colleague in New Jersey and I tried again, this time using "My Prom Night."

Team Problem Solving

Task: Authentic problem solving

Objective: To provide an interactive approach to problem solving and encourage group discussion

Author: Robin Lockhart, Assistant Professor, Midwestern State University—Wichita Falls, TX, robin.lockhart@mwsu.edu

Method: Asynchronous

Instructions

You have been assigned to a four-member group and provided with a private discussion area. Every three weeks, your instructor will post a problem for your group to solve. You have two weeks to solve the problem; it will then take a week to grade the results. The grade for your response will be based on individual participation and on the accuracy and depth of the final answer.

Activity Author's Note

I use these activities in my Internet-based courses. I use WebCT, so these activities are easily implemented. The size of the class in which I use this activity is generally thirty to forty students.

I average the scores of all the problems together and then use them for 10 percent of each student's final grade. In addition, I use the responses in the formation of the next problem.

Each of these activities is well received. The activities allow me to monitor students' understanding of course content and allow them to clarify concepts and form as a class. I never have any difficulty getting student interaction with these activities. I think the key is that the discussions are based on problems that the students generally need assistance in solving.

Pyramid

Task: Authentic task to interview a professional practicing in the student's field of study

Objective: To provide an innovative way for students to learn more about their field of study from a practicing professional

Author: J. Ana Donaldson, Ed.D., Walden University, ana.donaldson@waldenu.edu

Method: Asynchronous

Instructions

Contact an individual who is a professional in your field of study.

1. Complete the four pyramid areas based on e-mail contact with your selected individual.
2. Use the pyramid diagram as a guide to completing this activity.
3. Complete the pyramid's blocks in the following order:
   i. Job: Begin by completing the interviewee's job title and function.
   ii. Foundations: Based on e-mail inquiries, complete the bottom block with the individual's responses to the following items:
      • List the three things you value the most
      • What three words describe you
      • Describe your educational background
      • Identify three qualities you look for in an employee
      • List three qualities you expect from a boss
   iii. Transition 1: Describe the transitions that the individual experienced as they began their quest toward their current position.
   iv. Transition 2: Describe the final situation that resulted in the individual achieving their current position within the field.
      • Job:
      • Foundations
      • Transition 1:
      • Transition 2:
4. E-mail your final completed pyramid to your instructor as an attachment.

Activity Author's Note

This is a great tool for subsequent class discussion. Ask students what surprised them in the response. Another activity is to compare the responses on all replies for the foundation items. The transitional phases also help to remind students that networking, timing, and an element of serendipity often play a role in their professional future.

Social Responsibility

Task:	Authentic activity to involve students in their community
Objective:	To emphasize the importance of community and social responsibility
Author:	J. Ana Donaldson, Ed.D., Walden University, ana.donaldson@waldenu.edu
Method:	Asynchronous

Instructions

You will be assigned to a team of fellow classmates and a designated chat room for group communications. Your task will be as follows:

- Determine a problem within your community
- State the characteristics of targeted community members
- Define short-term and long-term solutions
- Provide a method for evaluation
- Document your efforts

Essential data gathering should include interviews with key individuals, existing reports, newspaper articles, and primary sources of information. It will be advantageous to document any previous attempts that have been made to solve this community problem.

At the end of the project, your team will submit a written report to the instructor.

Activity Author's Note

The final document from this project may be a letter to the mayor of the community, outlining the suggested solutions. The logical expansion of this task is to create the components necessary for writing a grant for funding. Once a problem is identified, determine if a grant opportunity exists. Assign the tasks for this activity around the elements required for grant submission. Many community organizations have grant resources that may support the class efforts.

Games and Simulations

By involving cyberstudents in activities that utilize games and simulations, real-life skills can be enhanced and learning can be made fun. SAGSET, the Society for the Advancement of Games and Simulations in Education and Training defines the terms simulations and games as follows: "Simulations and games are teaching and learning methods in which participants are directly involved in making decisions and learning from the outcomes of these. Their active, student centred nature means that they are memorable and highly motivating. They enable the exploration of the complex nature of the real world and interdisciplinary, interacting subjects as well as the more basic needs of understanding, doing and skills practice" (Society for the Advancement of Games and Simulations in Education and Training, 2002).

For the sake of this chapter, we make a distinction between video games and activities that are labeled games within the online environment. An activity that is categorized as a game includes tasks that provide an element of engagement, decision making, and knowledge acquisition from a new perspective. Activities that are categorized as simulations explore and replicate real-life situations. Role playing is an element of many simulations; in role playing, the student is asked to represent and experience a character type from an everyday experience.

Instruction through active involvement is the goal of an effective simulation. In this approach, participants are asked to look at real-life situations from "outside the box" and apply new approaches to the resolution of challenges or situations. In the optimal situation, students are provided opportunities to explore within a safe environment that allows them to share their views and explore new ideas without repercussions, in order to develop critical thinking and problem-solving skills.

The games in this chapter provide an entertaining approach to obtaining information and sharing it with class participants. The energy created by a game or simulation is visible in the quantity of discussion posts. These types of activities can create a situation that challenges and moves students to a new level of understanding.

All learners may not have prior experience with experiential learning so instructors need to be familiar with each student's knowledge level and experiences in order to introduce games or simulations in a manner that will reduce the potential for student discouragement (Burns & Gentry, 1998). Generational differences may also impact learners' comfort level with simulations and games (Prensky, 2001; Coates, 2007). However, learners who have been guided through the prior phases of engagement are usually prepared to handle the rigors of simulations and games.

CHARACTERISTICS OF AN EFFECTIVE GAME OR SIMULATION

Romme (2002, p. 1) states that simulations "create opportunities to build substantial synergy between learning to think in relevant theoretical frameworks and learning to deal with the complexity of actual settings." The checklist in Table 9.1 includes characteristics to look for when choosing or designing an activity. The ultimate evaluation criterion for this type of activity is whether the game or simulation asks the students to view their world from a new perspective that would not be possible within the standard learning environment.

Table 9.1. Checklist for an Effective Game or Simulation

	Yes/No	Comments
1. Is the student directly involved in making decisions and learning from the outcomes?		
2. Does the activity enable exploration of the complex nature of the real world?		
3. Does the game include tasks that provide elements of engagement, decision making, and knowledge acquisition from a new perspective?		
4. Does the simulation activity require students to role-play or to assume a new perspective?		
5. Does the game or simulation provide a safe environment for exploration?		

Table 9.2. Games and Simulations to Try

Activity	Asynchronous	Synchronous
Group Problem-Based Learning	✓	
Jilligan's Island	✓	
Spreadsheets	✓	
Virtual Field Trips	✓	
WebQuest	✓	

Group Problem-Based Learning

Task:	Online groups will prepare hardware, software, operating system, and peripheral device specifications for a simulated business
Objective:	To simulate a real-world situation and experience group problem-based learning
Author:	Charleen Worsham, Director of Instructional Technology and Distance Learning, Kilgore College, Kilgore, TX, charleen@kilgore.cc.tx.us
Method:	Asynchronous

Instructions

Problem Statement:
You have just been hired as the computer support expert in the information technology (IT) department at a new company—Spirit Designs, Inc. Your department has recently completed installation of Ethernet wiring throughout the new building.

The next task for the IT department will be to split into groups and prepare hardware, software, operating system, and peripheral device specifications for computers to be used by new employees due to arrive for work in three weeks.

You've heard that the boss is a penny pincher but that he doesn't have a problem spending money when it is justified. He likes to go first-class as long as the benefits outweigh the costs. Here are the assignments:

- *Group 1: The president of the company.* Although he has a background in graphic design, most of his time will be spent attending to the business matters of the company. He travels a lot to keep abreast of developments in the field of graphic design and Web design.
- *Group 2: The office manager.* She is responsible for all of the bookkeeping, payroll, accounts receivable, and accounts payable.
- *Group 3: The graphic designers.* The company already has several contracts for print-based jobs and Web page design.
- *Group 4: The IT department.* The IT director's goal is network and server management without anyone leaving his or her desk. The company needs at least one server, possibly more. It is imperative that the server remain up twenty-four hours a day, seven days a week.
- *Group 5: The president's fourteen-year-old son.* Like it or not, this type of assignment presents itself on occasion. He has recently discovered online gaming and is dyslexic.

About Problem-Based Learning:
If you haven't been faced with an assignment like this before, then welcome to the real world. Not all problems, projects, or assignments in life will provide you with all of the details you need, or the details may not be crystal clear. You will probably begin with many questions. Some questions will be answered by your instructor (see the Resources section of these instructions). Other questions you will have to answer on your own, with the help of your group members, or even with the help of other groups.

Working Together in an Online Course:
You may be wondering how to collaborate with each other online. First of all, I suggest that you select a group leader who will mediate your discussions and collect individual group members' contributions, disseminate them to the entire group, and post the completed project. You may want to use the "jigsaw method," in which each group member is given a specific piece of the problem to research, then reports back to the group. You may want to review the individual reports as a group in order to reach a consensus about the parts before putting them together to produce your final specifications.

The WebCT tools that you can use are WebCT e-mail, discussion board, chat, and the student presentation tool. One word of caution about the group presentations: be sure that two people aren't editing the same document at the same time, or you may lose your changes! Save your work on your local computer before uploading to WebCT. Your group will have a private area on the discussion board that other groups can't see. There will also be a common area set up for the entire class.

Tips on Chat: Try to set an agenda for the chat session; decide in advance what you want to discuss. Choose a group member to act as recorder, and have that person summarize what was decided during each chat and then post to either the discussion board or WebCT mail. This will remind everyone of what they are supposed to be doing and when they are supposed to have it done. Members who miss the chat will also be "in the loop" that way.

Group members in a course on Computer Supported Collaborative Learning (CSCL) at University of Texas–Austin composed the following list of the most important factors in the success of a collaborative activity. They divided their opinions into three categories. You may want to cover these items during your first meeting, whether it happens via chat, discussion board thread, or some other means.

Continued

What to Do at the Team Meeting
- Set a regular meeting time to avoid scheduling problems.
- Set and communicate an agenda before the team meeting.
- Assign specific responsibilities to each member.
- Set a due date earlier than the official due date for the final specifications so that team members can have time to comment on one another's work and discuss it.
- Verify each group member's understanding of assignments.

How to Communicate
- Allow enough time to get to know each other and share opinions.
- Offer honest opinions on others' work—including the quality and quantity of contributions to the group.
- Be a good listener.
- Be aware of the challenges that CSCL poses, including the delicate balance between (a) messages that are too short or use terms that may be unfamiliar to all participants, thereby increasing the likelihood of miscommunication and (b) messages that are verbose or unfocused on the subject matter, decreasing the likelihood that the entire message will be read by other group members pressed for time. (Funny that this is the longest of all the points made!)

Each Member's Obligations
- Keep teammates informed on the progress of the team assignment or individual tasks that might influence the team's work.
- Do what you are supposed to do when or, preferably, before you are supposed to do it.
- When acting in a leadership role for an assignment, ensure that the five points under "What to do at the team meeting" are covered.

Resources:
Use whatever resources you can find to gather pertinent information, including the following:

- Local stores
- Printed catalogues
- Internet resources, such as computer manufacturers or shopping portals
- The textbook
- Phone or in-person interviews

Be sure to list these sources in a reference section at the end of your report.

You may ask your instructor general questions regarding the scenario. These must be directed to the "Group Project Water Cooler" topic on the WebCT discussion board. Students may also communicate across groups in this area.

Report Format:
The final report must be in electronic form and posted to the Student Presentations section of WebCT for your group. The format and content of the final report is not prescribed; however, the scoring rubric will help you identify the essential elements you will need to score well.

Where Do We Start?
Perhaps the best place to begin is to perform a user analysis; determine what the person using your computer does. Think about the role that technology plays or might play in what that person does. This is the equivalent of a technology needs analysis at the user level. *Hint:* This information may come in handy when you justify your purchases.

Remember, it's a matter not simply of what you are proposing to buy, but also of why you need to buy it!

Above all, use your imagination and try to have a little fun with the assignment.

Assessment:
Instructions for completing the following assessments online will be provided at the beginning of the project.

A scoring rubric will be used to evaluate your completed project. Each student in the class and the instructor will score each group project. The following components will be scored:

- Overall computer specifications
- Coverage of system unit components
- Coverage of application software
- Coverage of input devices
- Coverage of output devices
- Coverage of storage devices
- Coverage of operating system and utility programs
- Appropriateness of specifications to end-user needs
- Budget and cost justification
- Writing clarity

Continued

In addition, students will also score themselves and each of their own group members based on cooperation, contribution, and participation.

Finally, you will be asked to share your reflections on the assignment, as follows:

- What I learned about buying a computer . . .
- What I learned about working with others in an online group . . .
- The time and effort to complete this assignment compared to what I learned was . . .

Activity Author's Note

This activity is based on the Student Handbook for COSC 1306, Web-Based Introduction to Computer Science. (Note: The assessment tools for this activity are presented in Tables 3.1, 3.2, and 3.3 earlier in this book.)

Jilligan's Island

Task: Team-building activity

Objective: To allow learners to experience team process and how to achieve group consensus

Author: Jill Jodrey, Instructional Developer, Simon Fraser University and Jones International University, Burnaby, BC, Canada, jajodrey@sfu.ca

Method: Asynchronous

Instructions:

We are all on a sinking boat, about to be stranded on a deserted island in the South Pacific. The lifeboat we have has limited space, so we're only able to bring a certain number of items with us. All of the communication instruments on the main ship have failed, so there are no working cell phones or laptops.

We can each bring one personal item with us, and it's completely up to each individual whether that item is something that will be useful to our total comfort on the deserted island. The lifeboat will hold the six of us, our one personal item each, and a total of eight other items.

Step One: Each of us must select our personal item and suggest five other items we feel will be necessary to our team survival. (The personal item can be anything of our choice, so it won't be voted on.) We must also provide reasons why we feel these items are necessary. Please also explain your reasons for choosing your personal item.

Step Two: We must collectively make a decision on the eight items that will come with us on our rescue boat.

The Forum will be our main means of communication. Please question one another on your choices, and try to sway others to your opinion. By Friday at midnight (our boat has a very slow leak:-)), we will have to come to a consensus; otherwise, it will be too late, and we'll perish on the sinking ship.

Continued

Activity Author's Note

I teach an online graduate-level education course. One of the issues I face each time I have a new intake of students is that it is difficult to find team-building activities that are specifically for virtual teams, so I adapted one that I've used in face-to-face classes for the Net. I post the activity in the Discussion Forum (asynchronous) on the first day of class (usually a Sunday), and set a deadline for about five days later. I also ask one student (privately) to be the "captain"—the person who compiles the list of all the suggested items. In the past, the captain has asked the other passengers to vote on this list and then provided the final list of items to everyone. This activity typically generates a lot of discussion, and students get to know each other in a friendly and fun environment.

Use of Spreadsheets in Managing a Business

Task: Simulation using spreadsheets

Objective: To allow students to apply spreadsheet skills and interactive online business communication skills in a simulated real-world situation

Author: Jim Morey, Instructor, Computer Information Systems Department, Mineral Area College, Park Hills, MO, JIMM@mail.mac.cc.mo.us

Method: Asynchronous

Instructions

You have been assigned to a team of four to six class members. The team must decide on a simulated business. On determining the business, you must depict how your business uses spreadsheets in managing the enterprise.

Typical spreadsheet uses include payroll, inventory catalogues, customer lists, income or sales projections, personnel lists, profit-and-loss statements, sales activity charts, work schedules, invoices, and expense reports, but any others that the team decides on can also be used.

Since the class is Web-based, team members must find ways to collaborate online. A private discussion area has been established for each team, using the courseware. Team members are also encouraged to use e-mail, telephones, and personal meetings—whatever is possible.

As a team member, you have to share responsibility for directing the team's activity. Members need to communicate their ideas and deliver on their portions of the project. In the end, all the spreadsheets will be put together in a presentation package. You will be notified of the due date for the final project.

Activity Author's Note

I use this online learning activity in an Excel spreadsheet applications course, CIS220, which I've been teaching at Mineral Area College, a small two-year state-supported college in southeast Missouri.

This exercise matches the "real" world in many ways. Team members within a company are often physically located at different sites. They collaborate through chat lines, e-mail messages, telephone conferences, personal meetings, and discussion boards. These collaboration and business communication skills can be learned in school. In addition, spreadsheet skills that are often learned through more traditional academic methods are applied in a simulated real-world business setting.

Virtual Field Trips

Task: Simulation visits to actual locations

Objective: To allow students to visit the world, going beyond the restrictions of geography

Author: Rita-Marie Conrad, Ph.D., Florida State University, Rita.Conrad@fsu.edu

Method: Asynchronous

Instructions

Visit one of the online locations on the list below, or select a site which provides a virtual tour that matches your interests and can be shared with the class. Report back to the group on your experiences. Your report should include the following:

- What did you learn that you didn't know before your visit?
- Why would you recommend or not recommend the site to other students?
- What would you like to explore if you visit this place in person?
- Find three other virtual field trips that you would recommend to the learning community.

Following are some suggested locations. See if you can find any additional virtual field trips.

- Great Art Museums of the World: www.ulaverne.edu/dlc/hum290/gratmus.html
- Virtual College Tours: http://www.campustours.com/
- China Virtual Tours: http://www.chinavista.com/travel/virtualtours.html
- Virtual Tour of Antarctica: http://astro.uchicago.edu/cara/vtour/
- Tower of London: http://www.toweroflondontour.com/
- Virtual Tour of the Ear: http://www.augie.edu/perry/ear/ear.htm
- Supreme Court Building: http://oyez.org/tour/tour
- Historical Tour of the White House: http://www.whitehouse.gov/history/whtour/
- Marshmallow Peeps Tours: http://www.marshmallowpeeps.com/peepsville.html

Activity Author's Note

Since sites change constantly, be sure to verify each site before sending your students on their journeys. The best way is to have them discover their own tour to share with other classmates.

WebQuest

Task:	Inquiry-oriented Internet exploration
Objective:	To provide students an opportunity to explore the Internet and practice the higher learning skills of analysis, synthesis, and evaluation
Developer:	Bernie Dodge, Ph.D., Professor of Educational Technology, San Diego State University, bdodge@mail.sdsu.edu
Method:	Asynchronous

This is an activity that can be developed by the instructor for student use or can be student-produced.

An overview, training materials, examples, and all other pertinent information is available at the WebQuest Page: http://webquest.sdsu.edu.

This site is hosted by the Educational Technology Department at San Diego State University and is updated regularly. Please suggest additions by writing bdodge@mail.sdsu.edu.

Author's Note

Bernie Dodge also had a WebQuest in a virtual environment (Second Life) around the topic of early California history. Resources such as Second Life open up the possibilities for simulations and gaming experiences.

Learner-Led Activities

Providing opportunities for learners to take the lead in preparing and delivering a successful instructional activity is the pinnacle of learner engagement. Learner-led activities provide a sense of empowerment that "is both a critical element and a desired outcome of participation in an online learning community" (Palloff & Pratt, 1999). This type of activity shifts the learner's mindset from viewing the instructor as the ultimate authority in the course to one of seeing himself or herself as a valued contributor to the learning environment. It is at this point that learners recognize that they are knowledge generators, not only for themselves but also for the community as a whole.

ACTIVITIES LED BY INDIVIDUALS VERSUS TEAMS

The phrase "safety in numbers" certainly is true for learner-led activities. It is recommended that learner-led activities be designed and presented by teams rather than individuals. Teams should be small (three to five members), in order to minimize the possibility of learners opting out of the activity; in addition, assessments that describe each team member's contribution to the activity will help ensure intragroup accountability. Team member evaluation, described in Chapter Three, is an excellent tool for measuring individual participation.

CONVEYING OUTCOMES

One of the most important aspects of student-led activities is to make sure that learners know what objectives the activity should accomplish. These expected outcomes should be stated in the syllabus, so that learners are aware of the requirements from the beginning of the course. Once basic outcomes have been conveyed, the learners can develop additional objectives for the activity if they wish.

CHOOSING THE TYPE OF ACTIVITY

There are five types of learning outcomes: intellectual skill, attitude, verbal information, cognitive strategy, and motor skill (Gagne, Briggs, & Wager, 1992). Of these five, the first three types lend themselves best to learner-led activities because there will be fewer barriers to success in an online environment. Learners should not be expected to lead the kind of complex activity that the last two types of learning outcomes could require.

Learner-led activities can be almost anything described thus far in this book or anything the learner can imagine. Presentations, discussions, role-playing activities, debates, and games can all be developed and led by learners instead of the instructor. The key is to make sure that expected learning outcomes are clearly stated and that learners are choosing the right type of activity based on the expressed objectives and expected outcomes.

It should always be assumed that learners are novice activity leaders; therefore, they should be encouraged to keep their activities simple from both pedagogical and technological perspectives. They should not introduce a new technology unless they feel confident that they can help their fellow community members to learn it.

ADEQUATE ORIENTATION AND PLANNING TIME

Students need ample time to develop the activities they lead. Following is a suggested approach:

1. Many learners may need to be oriented to the idea of leading a class activity. Start discussing the concept of learner-led activities at the beginning of the course and model various types of activities throughout the course.

2. Provide a detailed description of the activity and responsibilities of the learners in the syllabus.

3. Encourage learners to begin discussing the activities in teams after the first 25 percent of the course has been completed.

4. Provide time in the course calendar for learners to begin planning the activities around the middle of the semester.

5. Schedule time for the teams to discuss their activities with you, the instructor, several weeks before the team is scheduled to lead an activity. You will serve as counselor and consultant to the team as needed.

6. Remind teams that they are responsible for preparing the community for their activity by posting an announcement in the discussion board area or sending an e-mail to the entire class.

Table 10.1 provides some guidelines for creating effective learner-led activities.

Table 10.1. Checklist for an Effective Learner-Led Activity

	Yes/No	Comments
1. Are the objectives for the activity clearly stated in the syllabus?		
2. Is there a rubric for the grading of the activity?		
3. Is the concept of a learner-led activity introduced at least two weeks before learners begin planning it?		
4. Are learners provided several weeks to plan the activity?		
5. Does the topic allow a person or team to be creative in their choice and implementation of the activity?		
6. Does the participation grade include participation in the learner-led activities?		

WHAT DO LEARNERS THINK ABOUT LEARNER-LED ACTIVITIES?

Do learners actually value leading an activity in the way we as instructors hope they will? Here are some comments made by three different learners after leading an activity in one online course:

> This activity taught me to speak up. In the chat format, it is very easy to remain sort of anonymous. Being involved in this activity forced me to think, and to express my thoughts to all the group members. Hopefully, I will take that into my future courses. I learned so much from my fellow classmates. It was amazing to see the great care and preparation that went into the presentations and it really facilitated the learning process, not just for the presenters, but for the rest of the class as well.

> I would hope that most instructors these days would understand that more learning takes place in these type of activities than many times will in a more traditional way. Not to take away from the instructor-led portions of the classes at all, but the learner learns on many more levels when faced with this type of approach. I would say to an instructor that if their goal is to have the students truly understand what they are learning, this approach is much better. If the students have to be active participants, they will invest more of themselves, as well as time, into the course.

> Teaching this class will certainly influence how I listen and respond in future classes. A lot of work went into preparing the 45 minutes we were the teachers. It was important for us to capture the attention of the other students and not lose them from the start. In the future, I would not feel badly about telling others to limit their chatter when the instructors are trying to make a point. The shoe was on the other foot tonight, and while I enjoyed it, it must be very difficult to prepare for it every week. Your guidelines were straightforward and the restrictions were few. There have been many classes where I have participated in learner-led/directed activities that have failed miserably. One person did all the work while the others did nothing. Plus, often there is not enough time to prepare adequately. We were lucky

that we were the last group to present because we had more time to plan and perfect. Anyway, I guess what I am saying is that I would be very hesitant to advocate learner-led/directed activities in the future. I understand their value when done correctly, but have been involved in too many that were not implemented successfully.

EXAMPLES OF LEARNER-LED ACTIVITIES

This chapter contains four examples of actual learner-led activities. Learners in an actual course developed the first three examples that follow. Each of the first three examples includes the initial e-mail message that the leading team sent out to the rest of the learning community concerning the class topic they were covering. As you will see, each team used a combination of the communication tools available (both synchronous and asynchronous) and a variety of activity types to cover the topic. The fourth example is instructor-initiated but learner-led.

Learner-Led Activities: Example 1

Authors: Jessica Medina, Lorraine Stinson, Amber D. Brock, and Leslie Bendt

Hi Everyone!

Our project is simple and straightforward. There are just a few steps involved.

Step #1

Read our scenario prior to the class session on Wednesday night. It is posted on the General Class Discussion board. You will need to come to class ready to discuss possible solutions to our scenario. Be sure to finish the assigned readings for the week.

Step #2

On the night of our class presentation, we will ask you to go to the color iChat room to which you were assigned at the beginning of the course. There are separate iChat areas for red, blue, green, and white color rooms.

Step #3

Select one representative from your color group to present your responses during the last 30 minutes of class discussion. We will visit the color iChat rooms throughout your discussion.

Step #4

We ask that each group meet for the first 28 minutes of class, then return to the Main Room for a class presentation. One representative from each color group needs to be prepared to present their collective responses based on this timeline:

6:00–6:28 PM: Meet in your respective color iChat room for discussion.
6:30 PM: Return to the Main Room. Watch for us to initiate the discussion.
6:30 PM: Red Team, led by Marsha
6:36 PM: Green Team, led by Andrew
6:41 PM: Blue Team, led by Marcus
6:46 PM: White Team, led by Alija
6:50–7:00 PM: Wrap-up and closure

If you have any questions, please post them in the General Class Discussion area.

Thanks, Team One

Learner-Led Activities: Example 2

Authors: Terri Harrison, Amy Kinser, and Julie Abouelfatouh

Dear Classmates:

Here are the directions for this week's class. These directions are also posted on the class discussion board.

Before class, take the Team Roles Test at [URL provided]. We have been given permission to use this test as part of our lesson by the Web site authors.

There are specific directions on the Web page, but basically you have 20 points to disperse in each section. You can rate each item from 0 to 20, but the total for each section has to equal 20 points. You must have two windows open—one to check your e-mail and get the password and one where you are taking the test. The warning on the Web page says: DON'T CLOSE THIS PAGE when you have answered the questions! You get your code page here in this program! If you close you cannot get your results!

Here is an example:

The most characteristic for me when it comes to team work is that I

- a. organize others' work on the team (4 pts)
- b. continually search for information and contacts that the team needs (2 pts)
- c. see to it that everyone has something to do, and coordinate different activities (1 pt)
- d. am capable of carrying out those ideas that the team has decided on (4 pts)
- e. see to it that people feel good and feel at home on the team (0 pts)
- f. use my force and strength to push the team forward (5 pts)
- g. create ideas that the team needs (2 pts)
- h. think carefully and warn about developments that go wrong (2 pts)

Total = 20 points

The results discuss the eight different roles and tell you which roles you are strongest and weakest in.

Questions to discuss this week in your group areas:

1. Discuss the results of the test with your group.
   - What were your strongest areas?
   - What were your weakest areas?
   - Are there any significant similarities or differences in the results?

2. Did you feel the results were accurate? How will this affect your group behavior?
3. How do the eight roles discussed in the results of the test relate to the roles discussed in the text?
4. Why do you think knowing about group roles is important?

Begin your discussion no later than Monday night. One member of our team will facilitate your discussion. Be prepared to summarize your discussion during Thursday's chat session.

Learner-Led Activities: Example 3

Authors: Leslie Gramaglia, Judy A. Harris, Johann Juste, Bill Secrest, and Kim Parker

LESSON PLAN
TEAM 2

I. Introduction

Rather than indulge in skills-oriented exercises, we have decided to adopt a different approach to discussing organizational design. Now that you have read the text and the two assigned articles, we are interested in finding out the OPINIONS you have now developed on this topic.

To gauge your opinions, we ask you to open up a new browser window and record your responses to ten organizational design questions we have placed on a Web site. We will go through these questions one by one and ask you to cast your votes. When you have finished with each question, you (and everyone else in the class) will be able to press a button and see the class's responses—instantaneously!

In order to avoid flooding the server when voting, we ask that you pick a random number between 1 and 10 after reading each question, count to that number, and then click your mouse.

The results should be quite meaningful, since the Web site is set up so you can vote only once on any given question.

Roughly an hour's time gives us only five or six minutes per question, so we expect to move through the poll rather fast. What we will do is use your responses as a springboard for a brief discussion. All five team members will rotate the moderating duties, commenting and leading discussion on two questions each.

If you have any questions or comments as we go along, please let us know.

II. Questions

1. The author of the text cites five major factors where organizational design intersects with leadership. In your opinion, which one is the most significant?

   a. Background factors
   b. Leadership philosophy
   c. Organizational design decisions
   d. Organizational culture
   e. Organizational results

2. The authors discuss five "hybrid" models of organization. In your opinion, which one do you think is the most useful for today's workplace?

   a. Federalist
   b. Shamrock
   c. Doughnut
   d. Clan
   e. Spaghetti

3. Among the "hybrid" models of organization, which one do you predict will become most popular in the next two decades?

   a. Federalist
   b. Shamrock
   c. Doughnut
   d. Clan
   e. Spaghetti

4. The author of the text cites four key systems that have an impact on organizational design. In your opinion, which one is the most significant?

   a. Hiring
   b. Training
   c. Reward
   d. Information processing/sharing

5. The authors of one article discuss the analytical approach to leadership and organizational design. In your opinion, what is the biggest flaw of this approach?

   a. Fixing goals too firmly
   b. Too much trust in research, numbers, and reasoned analysis
   c. Allowing outside demands to drive organizational direction
   d. An overly "scientific" approach
   e. Emphasizing the predictable over the unpredictable

Continued

6. The author of the other article speaks of the need for leaders to take an interpretive approach to organizational design. In your opinion, which of the following groups is the most important for the interpretive leader to consult in decision making?

a. Employees
b. Customers
c. Vendors
d. Management in identical or similar organizations
e. Consultants/academics

7. In your opinion, which of the following is the most important net result of proper interpretive leadership?

a. Satisfied employees/customers
b. Higher profit margins
c. Recognition for innovation
d. Open climate for new ideas and thinking
e. Increased adaptability to change

8. The author of one article says that for businesses to survive, they must "manage themselves around the idea of process"—making workers understand how their efforts affect a larger whole. Which of the following helps workers best understand process?

a. Specialized education or training
b. Collaborative atmosphere
c. Rotating tasks
d. Exposing all employees to customer service
e. Integrating workers and leaders in decision making

9. What, in your opinion, is the biggest hindrance to implementing a process orientation in an organization?

a. Orientation toward profit
b. Traditional neglect of the customer
c. Managers unwilling to share power
d. General tendency to resist change
e. Poor communication climate

10. In your opinion, what is the most compelling reason for organizations to adopt a process orientation?

a. Greater competitiveness
b. Increased worker satisfaction
c. Improved collaborative spirit
d. Encouraging action
e. Encouraging innovation

III. Closing and Thanks

We appreciate the class participating in this exercise and hope it has been informative and entertaining for everyone.

We will leave the poll results up for anyone who wishes to take a second look at them.

If you have any further questions about anything discussed or how to set up an interactive poll of your own, let us know via e-mail or the faculty office.

Again, our thanks and have a great evening.

Author: Sharon Calhoon, Ph.D., Indiana University, Kokomo; scalhoon@iuk.edu

Instructions

E-mail discussion is run just like a classroom discussion, except that you may participate at a time that is convenient for you. Once you have read the assigned material, send any questions or comments you have for discussion to the discussion forum. I DO NOT run this discussion—you do! You are responsible for asking questions, for answering others' questions, for generating discussion topics, and for ensuring that the discussion remains interesting, learning-focused, and collegial. Please have your discussion for the week completed by Monday evening. [*Note:* This is if the new unit begins Wednesday.] Messages sent right before a new unit begins do not count toward your discussion grade. This way we will have a day to wrap up any loose ends in the discussion before the new unit begins.

Your participation will be graded on the following scale:

- *3 points:* Fully participated; questions and comments were insightful and to the point; recognized and respected others' rights. You must participate in the discussion on at least two separate days during the week in order to receive three points.
- *2 points:* Participated occasionally or submissions were not thoughtful or well-developed; comments and questions were generally appropriate but not well thought out or did not demonstrate knowledge of or interest in the reading assignment.
- *1 point:* Participation was brief and consisted only of agreement with others' comments, or comments were rude or otherwise inappropriate.

Activity Author's Note

I do not structure the discussion. When I let them talk about what is interesting or confusing to them, they become responsible for their learning and they seem to get a lot more out of the discussion. Many students have said to me, "I thought I understood the chapter quite well until someone asked a question. I'd have to go back and find the answer, and then I'd realize what I missed the first time through." When they structure the discussion, I learn more about what I need to do to help them learn the material. I assure them that I will monitor their discussion frequently to make sure they aren't leading one another astray. Because I can't always tell when they are unable to come up with an answer, I encourage them to alert me (by writing directly to me) when they have tried to help one another understand something but still are confused. Otherwise, I stay out of the discussion. When I do write something on a topic, my submission seems to serve as a "closing" statement ("The Expert has spoken!"), whether I intend it to or not.

I require students to participate on two separate days to ensure that it's really a discussion. They must respond to one another's questions and answers and not just drop in, write a few lines, and then drop out.

E-mail discussion counts for a significant portion of the final grade, which certainly helps motivate students to participate. Participation is graded on a weekly (or per-unit) basis. Before calculating the final grade, I drop the lowest participation score (in case students have problems with technology, are ill, and so forth). This helps to eliminate students' complaints about not being able to get points because of circumstances beyond their control.

References

Bloom, B. S. (1956). *Taxonomy of educational objectives: The classification of educational goals.* New York: Longman.

Boettcher, J., & Conrad, R. M. (2010). *The online teaching survival guide: Simple and practical pedagogical tips.* San Francisco: Jossey-Bass.

Bornstein, M. H., & Bruner, J. S. (1989). On interaction. In M. H. Bornstein & J. S. Bruner (Eds.), *Interaction in human development.* Hillsdale, NJ: Erlbaum.

Bruner, J. (1966). *Toward a theory of instruction.* Cambridge, MA: Harvard University Press.

Burns, A. C., & Gentry, J. W. (1998). Motivating students to engage in experiential learning: A tension-to-learn theory. *Simulation and Gaming, 29,* 133–151.

Chamberlain, R., & Vrasidas, C. (2001). Creating engaging online instruction. *Proceedings of the 17th Annual Conference on Distance Teaching and Learning.* Madison, WI: University of Wisconsin System. 79–83.

Coates, J. (2007). *Generational learning styles.* River Falls, WI: LERN Books.

Collison, G., Elbaum, B., Haavind, S., & Tinker, R. (2000). *Facilitating online learning: Effective strategies for moderators.* Madison, WI: Atwood.

Cross, J. (2007). *Informal learning: Rediscovering the natural pathways that inspire innovation and performance.* San Francisco: Jossey-Bass.

Dewey, J. (1997). *Democracy and education: An introduction to the philosophy of education.* New York: The Free Press. (Original work published 1916)

Dick, W., Carey, L., & Carey, J. (2009). *The systematic design of instruction* (7th ed.). Boston: Addison-Wesley.

Draves, W. (2000). *Teaching online.* River Falls, WI: LERN Books.

Draves, W. (2009). *Advanced teaching online.* River Falls, WI: LERN Books.

Driscoll, M. P. (2005). *Psychology of learning for instruction* (3rd ed.). Boston: Allyn & Bacon.

Gagne, R., Briggs, L., & Wager, W. (1992). *Principles of instructional design* (4th ed.). Fort Worth, TX: Harcourt Brace Jovanovich.

Gagne, R. M., & Driscoll, M. P. (1988). *Essentials of learning for instruction* (2nd ed.). Boston: Allyn & Bacon.

Harasim, L. H., Hiltz, R., Teles, L., & Turoff, M. (1996). *Learning networks: A field guide to teaching and learning online*. Cambridge, MA: MIT Press.

Jeong, A. (2001–2009). *Discussion analysis tool.* http://myweb.fsu.edu/ajeong/dat/. Updated Nov. 3, 2009.

Jeong, A. (2003). Sequential analysis of group interaction and critical thinking in online threaded discussions. *American Journal of Distance Education, 17*(1), 25–43.

Johnson, M. (October 1998). *Article for School Times* [Online]. Retrieved 2/02/00. Available: http://www.ash.udel.edu/incoming/mjohnson/article1.html.

Kearsley, G. (2000). *Online education: Learning and teaching in cyberspace*. Belmont, CA: Wadsworth/Thomson Learning.

Knowles, M. (1980). *The modern practice of adult education: From pedagogy to andragogy* (2nd ed.). New York: Association Press.

Mentkowski, M., & Associates. (2000). *Learning that lasts: Integrating learning, development, and performance in college and beyond*. San Francisco: Jossey-Bass.

Merriam, S. B., Caffarella, R. S., & Baumgartner, L. M. (2007). *Learning in adulthood: A comprehensive guide* (3rd ed.). San Francisco: Jossey-Bass.

Meyer, K. (2002). *Quality in distance education: Focus on on-line learning*. San Francisco: Jossey-Bass.

Mezirow, J. (1991). *Transformative dimensions of adult learning*. San Francisco: Jossey-Bass.

Moore, M., & Kearsley, G. (2004). *Distance education: A systems view*. Belmont, CA: Wadsworth.

Norris, D., Mason, J., & Lefrere, P. (2003). *Transforming e-knowledge*. Ann Arbor, MI: Society for College and University Planning.

Oosterhoff, A., Conrad, R., & Ely, D. (2008). *Assessing learners online*. Upper Saddle River, NJ: Pearson.

Palloff, R. M., & Pratt, K. (1999). *Building learning communities in cyberspace: Effective strategies for the online classroom*. San Francisco: Jossey-Bass.

Palloff, R. M., & Pratt, K. (2001). *Lessons from the cyberspace classroom: The realities of online teaching*. San Francisco: Jossey-Bass.

Palloff, R. M., & Pratt, K. (2003). *The virtual student: A profile and guide to working with online learners*. San Francisco: Jossey-Bass.

Palloff, R. M., & Pratt, K. (2007). *Building online learning communities: Effective strategies for the virtual classroom*. San Francisco: Jossey-Bass.

Piaget, J. (1969). *The mechanisms of perception*. London: Routledge & Kegan Paul.

Prensky, M. (2001). *Digital game-based learning*. New York: McGraw-Hill.

Romme, G. L. (2002). *Microworlds for management education and learning* [Online]. Available: http://www.business.ltsn.ac.uk/events/BEST%202002/Papers/Romme.PDF.

Salmon, G. (2002). *e-tivities: The key to active online learning*. London: Kogan Page.

Silberman, M., with K. Lawson (1995). *101 ways to make training active*. San Francisco: Pfeiffer.

Simonson M., Smaldino, S., Albright, M., & Zvacek, S. (2008). *Teaching and learning at a distance: Foundations of distance learning* (4th ed.). Upper Saddle River, NJ: Prentice Hall.

Smith, P. L., & Ragan, T. J. (1999). *Instructional design* (2nd ed.). Upper Saddle River, NJ: Prentice Hall.

Society for the Advancement of Games and Simulations in Education and Training (2002). The Society for the Advancement of Games and Simulations for Education and Training—Homepage [Online]. Available: http://www.simulations.co.uk/sagset/sagset2.htm.

Thorpe, M. (2008). Effective online interaction: Mapping course design to bridge from research to practice. *Australian Journal of Educational Technology, 24*(1), 57–72.

Vygotsky, L. S. (1981). The genesis of higher mental functions. In J. V. Wertsch (Ed.), *The concepts of activity in Soviet psychology*. Armonk, NY: Sharpe.

Watson, G., & Groh, S. (2001). Faculty mentoring faculty. In Duch, B., Groh, S., & Allen, D. (Eds.), *The power of problem-based learning*. Sterling, VA: Stylus.

Wedemeyer, C. (1981). *Learning at the back door*. Madison: University of Wisconsin Press.

Weigel, V. B. (2002). *Deep learning for a digital age*. San Francisco: Jossey-Bass.

Weimer, M. (2002). *Learner-centered teaching*. San Francisco: Jossey-Bass.

West, J., & West M. (2009). *Using wikis for online collaboration*. San Francisco: Jossey-Bass.

Woo, Y., & Reeves, T. (2007). Meaningful interaction in web-based learning: A social constructivist interpretation. *Internet and Higher Education, 10*, 15–25.

INDEX

Page references followed by *fig* indicate an illustrated figure; followed by *t* indicated a table; followed by *e* indicate an exhibit.

A

Group Contract, 73–74; Group Problem-Based Learning game/simulation, 104–108; How's My Driving?, 75–76; I Can Find That, 45; I Didn't Know That, 87; IRAs (Insights, Resource Sharing, and Applications), 88; Jilligan's Island game/simulation, 109–110; Library Search, 44; Lineup, 56; Medieval Shield, 77; More Words to Lead By, 89; Name That Movie, 58; One Word, 59; Picture, 90; Portrait, 60; Progressive Project, 78; Pyramid, 99; Room with a View, 61; Scavenger Hunt, 46; Skills Survey, 42; Snowball, 62; Social Responsibility, 100; Structured Discussion, 80; Summary Words, 91; Syllabus Quiz, 47; Team Problem Solving, 98; Things, 63; Truths and Lies, 64; Use of Spreadsheets in Managing a Business, 111; Virtual Field Trips game/simulation, 112; WebQuest, 113; What Kind of Animal?, 65; Why Are We Together?, 66. *See also* Synchronous activities

Asynchronous communication: description, 25; group reporting on, 19; tools used for, 23t–24t

Authentic activities: Case Study, 95; Celebrity Chat, 96; characteristics of effective, 93; checklist for effective, 94t; Cross-Region Discussion, 97; meaningful experiences through, 92; Pyramid, 99; Social Responsibility, 100; suggestions for, 94t; Team Problem Solving, 98

B

Bartelson, G., 78
Baumgartner, L. M., 21

Bendt, L., 119
Bingo activity, 54
Blog communication, 23t
Bloom, B. S., 18, 28
Bloom's taxonomy, 18, 28
Boettcher, J., 68
Brainstorming, 19
Briggs, L., 115
Brock, A. D., 119
Brooks, R. F., 37
Bruner, J., 2
Bumper Sticker activity, 85
Burns, A. C., 102

C

Caffarella, R. S., 21
Calhoon, S., 126
Carey, J., 28
Carey, L., 28
Case Study activity, 95
CD-ROMs, 22, 23t
Celebrity Chat activity, 96
Chat rooms, 23t
Christison, C., 61
Classmate Quiz activity, 55
Classroom-based activities: considerations for online adaption of, 18–19; examples of easy online conversion of, 19–20
Coates, J., 102
Collaboration: engaged learning as process of, 6; peer partnership and team, 67–80, 104–110
Collaborator learner role: activity example for, 13t; description of, 9t, 10, 11
Collison, G., 3, 5
Communication tools: asynchronous, 19, 25; characteristics of specific, 22, 23t–24t; choosing effective, 21–22,

25–26; considerations for selecting, 26; synchronous, 19, 25, 26; WebCT, 98, 105

Community member/challenger instructor role: activity example for, 13*t*; description of, 9*t*, 10, 11

Computer Supported Collaborative Learning (CSCL) [University of Texas—Austin], 105–108

Conrad, R.-M., 27, 37, 57, 62, 66, 68, 84, 112

Constructivism: description of, 3; on learner engagement, 3–4

Content construction, 3

Contest of the Week activity, 71

Cooperator learner role: activity example for, 12*t*; description of, 9*t*, 10, 11

Crane, K. R., 44

Critical Insight activity, 86

Critical thinking assessment, 28–29

Cross, J., 21

Cross-Region Discussion activity, 97

D

Darden, D., 97

Dereshiwsky, M. I., 73, 89

Designing online engagement: adapting classroom-based activities for, 18–20; choosing an effective communication tool, 21–26; considerations for, 17–18; to meet the needs of online learners, 20–21

Dewey, J., 1

Dick, W., 28

Discussion activities: analysis tools for assessing, 29; developing effective, 21

Discussion boards, 23*t*

Distance learners. *See* Online learners

Dodge, B., 113

Donaldson, J. A., 45, 56, 63, 77, 90, 91, 96, 99, 100

Drag and Drop activity, 43

Draves, W., 6, 43

Driscoll, M. P., 7

Dyad activities: Contest of the Week, 71; Dyad Debate, 72; forming dyads for, 67; moving to teams from, 68–69; Progressive Project, 78. *See also* Team activities

Dyad Debate activity, 72

E

E-mail communication, 23*t*

Elbaum, B., 3, 5

Elluminate, 22

Ely, D., 27

Engaged learning: as collaborative learning process, 6; constructivism on, 3–4; description of, 1; external learning conditions to maximize, 7; "IRA approach" to facilitate, 88; learning theorists on, 1–2; PBL (problem-based learning) extension of, 2–3, 104–108. *See also* Learning; Online engaged learning

Engaged learning model, 4*fig*

F

Facebook sites, 22

Facilitator instructor role: activity example for, 13*t*; description of, 9*t*, 10, 11

Farrior, E., 79

Faulk, D. R., 72, 80

Fax communication, 24*t*

Feedback: evaluating critical thinking, 28–29; need for informative, 7

Florida State University, 37

One Word, 59; Portrait, 60; Room
with a View, 61; Snowball, 62;
suggestions for, 53t; Things, 63;
Truths and Lies, 64; What Kind
of Animal?, 65; Why Are We
Together?, 66
Online learner skills: activities for
building, 40t–47; issues to consider
for building, 38–39
Online learners: building skills in using
necessary tools, 38–47; cooperator
role of, 9t, 10, 11, 12t; designing to
meet needs of, 20–21; generational
differences of, 21; guiding online
engagement by, 7–11; individual
learning styles of, 39; initiator/partner
role of, 9t, 10, 11, 13t; key engaged
learning elements for, 6; newcomer
role of, 8, 9t, 10, 11, 12t; providing
meaningful experiences to, 92; self-
motivation importance for, 6–7;
"teachable moments" of, 25. *See also*
Learners
Oosterhoff, A., 27
Ostrow, C. L., 95
Overnight mail communication, 24t

P

Pair Share activity, 12t
Palloff, R. M., 5, 6, 17, 20, 28, 92, 114
Palm, D., 58
Parker, K., 122
Peer partnerships activities: checklist for
effective team activity, 69t; Contest of
the Week, 71; Dyad Debate, 72;
forming dyads for, 67; Group
Contract, 73–74; Group Problem-
Based Learning game/simulation,
104–108; How's My Driving?, 75–76;
issues to consider during, 67–68;

Jilligan's Island game/simulation, 109–
110; Medieval Shield, 77; moving
dyads to teams, 68–69; Progressive
Project, 78; Structured Chat, 79;
Structured Discussion, 80; suggestions
for, 70t
Phases of Engagement framework:
appropriate activities for, 11, 12t–13t,
19; description of each phase, 8,
10–11; learner/instructor roles and
process of, 9t. *See also* Online engaged
learning
Phone communication, 24t
Piaget, J., 2
Picture activity, 90
Portrait activity, 60
Pratt, K., 5, 6, 17, 20, 29, 92, 114
Prensky, M., 102
Problem-based learning (PBL):
description of, 2–3; Group Problem-
Based Learning game/simulation,
104–108
Professional learning networks (PLNs),
22
Progressive Project activity, 78
Project rubric, 31t–32t
Proof of Performance (Nelles), 86
Pyramid activity, 99

R

Ragan, T. J., 3, 19
Reeves, T., 5
Reflective activities: Aha!, 84; Bumper
Sticker, 85; characteristics of an
effective, 82; checklist for an effective,
83t; Critical Insight, 86; I Didn't
Know That, 87; IRAs (Insights,
Resource Sharing, and Applications),
88; issues to consider for, 81–82; More
Words to Lead By, 89; Picture, 90;

suggestions for, 83t; Summary Words, 91

Reflective Diary Activity, 36e

Reflective self-assessments: journaling for, 34, 36e; transformative learning function of, 34, 37

Reigel, D., 58

Romme, G. L., 102

Room with a View activity, 61

Rubrics: constructing activity, 30; definition of, 29–30; example of project, 31t–32t; example of team, 33t. *See also* Assessments

S

Salmon, G., 5, 17

Scavenger Hunt activity, 46

Schwartz, S. E., 55, 71, 87

Searcey, D., 65

Second Life, 23t, 113

Secrest, B., 122

Self-assessments: example of activity for, 34t; reflective, 34, 36e–37; Skills Survey activity, 42

Silberman, M., 85

Simonson, M., 6

Simulations. *See* Games and simulations

Skill-building activities: Are You Ready for Learning Online?, 41; Drag and Drop, 43; I Can Find That, 45; Library Search, 44; listed, 40t; Scavenger Hunt, 46; Skills Survey, 42; Syllabus Quiz, 47

Skills Survey activity, 42

Skype, 23t

Smaldino, S., 6, 85

Smith, P. L., 3, 19

Snowball activity, 62

Social negotiator instructor role: activity example for, 12t; description of, 8, 9t, 10, 11

Social networking activities, 22

Social presence, 51

Social Responsibility activity, 100

Society for the Advancement of Games and Simulations in Education and Training (SAGSET), 101

Stinson, L., 119

Structural engineer instructor role: activity example for, 12t; description of, 9t, 10, 11

Structured Chat activity, 79

Structured Discussion activity, 80

Students. *See* Online learners

Summary Words activity, 13t, 91

Swart, S. L., 46

Syllabus: expected activity outcomes stated in, 115; learner-led activity objectives stated in, 116t; Syllabus Quiz activity on, 47

Synchronous activities: Celebrity Chat, 96; Contest of the Week, 71; Group Contract, 73–74; How's My Driving?, 75–76; Lineup, 56; Lost in Space, 57; Medieval Shield, 77; One Word, 59; Snowball, 62; Structured Chat, 79; Summary Words, 91; Truths and Lies, 64; Why Are We Together?, 66. *See also* Asynchronous activities

Synchronous communication: description of, 25, 26; group reporting on, 19; tools for, 23t–24t

T

"Teachable moments," 25

Team activities: checklist for effective, 69t; considerations for assigning, 68–69; Group Contract, 73–74; Group Problem-Based Learning game/simulation, 104–108; How's My Driving?, 75–76; intragroup

More Resources from the Jossey-Bass Online Teaching and Learning Series!

The Essential Online Teaching and Learning Tool Kit

ISBN: 1118027213 | Price: $105.00 USD

Online teaching and learning is expanding rapidly on campuses everywhere, yet educators often lack the resources they need to translate their courses to an online environment. We've taken the guesswork out of assembling the professional development library you need, offering hand-picked resources that cover all of your online teaching and learning needs.

Tool kit includes:

Learning In Real Time by Jonathan E. Finkelstein
Engaging the Online Learner by Rita-Marie Conrad and
　J. Ana Donaldson
Assessing the Online Learner by Rena M. Palloff and Keith Pratt
Conquering the Content by Robin M. Smith
Creating a Sense of Presence Online by Rosemary M. Lehman and Simone C. O. Conceicao

> **You save 25%**
> on **all titles** when
> you buy the
> complete
> tool kit!

Join The Jossey-Bass Online Teaching and Learning Community!

The Jossey-Bass Online Teaching and Learning (OTL) Conference ONLINE

Based on the popular series of Jossey-Bass guide-books on online teaching and learning, the OTL Conference Online brings all of the books' authors – as well as a community of hundreds of professionals worldwide – right to your desktop for interactive online sessions, discussions, hands-on learning, strategy swapping, and networking. The conference takes place every October, so mark your calendars in advance!

The Jossey-Bass OTL Community Website

The learning continues all year round at the Jossey-Bass OTL community website. You'll be the first to know about details of the upcoming OTL conference, receive information on the newest professional development resources from Jossey-Bass, learn about the latest free podcasts and video clips from your favorite authors and experts, and discover much more! You can also sign up for the *OTL Update*, a FREE monthly e-newsletter full of the latest tips and tricks from experts in the field – just visit the site and sign up today!

Join our community and be the first to know about the final dates and details of our next OTL Conference Online by visiting **www.onlineteachingandlearning.com.**